The Google Ad Grants

Playbook

The Definitive Guide To
Breakthrough Nonprofit Growth...
On Google's Dime

Josh Barsch & Steve L. Isaacs

ISBN 978-1539873471

CONTENTS

PREFACE

(Or, "Who Knew Dinosaur Erotica Was More Popular Than Free Money?")

Writing books these days is tough. Tougher than it was even, say, 10 years ago, before Borders and Waldenbooks and who knows how many other big bookstore chains went belly-up. The conventional wisdom declares that almost no one reads books anymore anyway, and those who do prefer to read 'em on Kindles or iPads or some other kind of device.

But it's not just that. Take a spin through the deep nooks and crannies of the Amazon Kindle store, and you're left with a single thought that goes something like this: "Wow … there's a book about *everything* if you look hard enough." Decades after the floodgates of digital publishing were flung open to the masses, you can find e-books on everything from how to care for your pet frog (there are dozens of these) to the most obscure, esoteric fan fiction to – wait for it – dinosaur erotica. Yes, dinosaur erotica: bodice-rippers unique in that the bodice-ripping is being done by a Triceratops. I've never read them, but Steve says he's hooked and can't wait until the new "Brontosauruses In Heat" series is released. **(Note from Josh: See, Steve, this is what happens when you make me write the preface all by myself)**.

So I'm not at all kidding when I say that this book nearly never got written, because – well, honestly, we just kind of assumed someone else had already written it. I mean, the Google Ad Grants program is NOT new; it's been around for over a decade. At our agency, StraightForward Interactive, Steve and I have managed 100-plus Google Ad Grants account over that time. We've developed some serious go-to strategies, answered the same 50 questions about 250 times and built thousands of Google advertising campaigns with literally millions of ads and keywords.

In short: This stuff is kinda "old hat" for us, and when something is old hat, your brain starts assuming that it's old hat for everyone else, too. Apparently, it's not. I was putting some Ad Grants management guidelines together for a new hire at our agency, and after pounding the keys for a couple days straight, I wondered whether it'd be worth it to go the extra mile and turn my notes into a book. It wouldn't be the only Ad Grants book on the market, but if I'd already written it all up, why not toss it out on the market?

As it turned out, it *was* the only Google Ad Grants book on the market – or at least the only book of its kind. Sure, you can find a few free e-books with 10 or 15 pages breathlessly rehashing the Ad Grants program guidelines, but the detailed guide you have here is, surprisingly enough, the first of its kind. I still can't believe it's taken 10 years for a guide like this to come out (although, to be fair, it took the dinosaur erotica people at least 65 million years since the most recent interlude of real-life Jurassic lovemaking to write about that, so I guess we were quicker to our punch than they were to theirs).

So it's with genuine excitement that we wrote this book, and we're even more excited and grateful that you bought it. How many of us get the chance to be absolutely, irrefutably FIRST to any party these days? It's a little nerve-wracking, honestly, but far outweighed by awesomeness. Who knows? Maybe we'll end up being the Strunk & White of Google Ad Grants. (I'll be Strunk. Steve can be White. "Strunk" just sounds more powerful.)

Actually, we'll be happy if we just outsell "Taken by the T-Rex," and thanks to you, we're one sale closer to doing that.

Hope you enjoy the book as much as we enjoyed writing it.

Your pals,
Josh & Steve

INTRODUCTION

(Or, "What the Heck Is Google Ad Grants, Anyway?")

Let's get right down to brass tacks, then.

Google Ad Grants – known simply as "Google Grants" prior to 2015 – is a 13-year-old program that gives $10,000 per month in free advertising to 501(c)(3) nonprofits in the United States and to equivalent organizations in 50-plus other countries around the globe.

It's an in-kind grant, delivered to each nonprofit inside a specially created advertising account via Google AdWords, Google's flagship advertising program (which is, and always has been, Google's primary source of revenue). The account comes loaded with $329 per day worth of advertising credit, and once you've got one, you're ready to rock and roll.

If you've worked in the nonprofit world for any length of time and are familiar with the Sisyphean task of applying for grant money, you're in for a pleasant surprise. A Google Ad Grant takes about 15 minutes to sign up for and is obscenely easy to get. It's also perpetual: Once you've signed up and been approved, the free advertising money is yours forever, provided you don't violate the program policies (there are a lot of those, and we'll cover them later) and provided Google doesn't wake up one day and decide to end the entire program (don't hold your breath; it's a major PR feather in Google's cap).

And unless your nonprofit falls into one of a handful of ineligible categories (hospitals/medical groups, schools, child-care centers or government-funded entities) or your organization has received an Ad Grant previously but had it revoked for violating the above-referenced policies, your acceptance into the program is all but assured.

Sounds simple, right?

Well … not exactly.

A BRAND-NEW CADILLAC WITH NO ENGINE

Or, "Why Google Ad Grants Is Wonderful, but Less Wonderful Than You Think, yet Still Undoubtedly Wonderful")

We know that the Ad Grants program is lucrative, it's easy to get into, and unless you screw it up, it's yours forever once you're in.

So every nonprofit on Earth must have one, right?

Nope. Despite the above, most nonprofits have still never heard of the Ad Grants program, and even fewer have signed up and received it. And even among the tiny sliver of nonprofits that have been awarded the Ad Grant, only a fraction of a percent of them make full use of it.

Why, after 13 years, is Google Ad Grants still little-known and severely underused by the nonprofit world? Very simple: Using Google Ad Grants is tricky. There's not just one catch; there's a ton of 'em.

Our best analogy is this: If someone offered you a new Cadillac free of charge, would you take it? No taxes, no fees, no nothing – just a brand-new Cadillac dropped in your driveway. Of course you would.

But what if you popped the hood on your new car, and everything was shiny and perfect except for one thing: There was a giant hole where the engine's supposed to be.

Well, that's a problem. I mean, it's not a dealbreaker, really; it's still a beautiful new ride. But it's definitely a problem. The damn thing isn't any good to you until you can drive it around, and without an engine, you definitely cannot drive it around.

But let's say it costs you $6,000 to put an engine in it. You weren't expecting that expense, but you spent $6,000, and now your beautiful new Cadillac is street-ready and has a market value of $55,000. And it cost you exactly $6,000.

Still worth it? Absolutely, an incredible steal. BUT -- It's still not quite the same as totally free.

This is precisely the hand you're dealt with Google Ad Grants. Google comes up to you and says, "Hey there, Forward-Thinking Nonprofit Leader, how'd you like $10,000 in free advertising per month?" And you, correctly identified as a forward-thinking nonprofit leader, answer: "Uh, absolutely I would. I'm of sound mind. I'd be a fool to not want this excellent thing you're offering." And Google says, "OK, it's yours! Enjoy!"

And then you get back to your office with your shiny new grant, and you're ready to fire it up, but there's one problem: Try as you might, you're not actually spending any of it. You have $329 per day to spend, and you're spending only $10 or $15 of that cash each day. What's the problem?

The problem is that a Google Ad Grant arrives with no engine. It doesn't spend money by itself; instead, it needs an engine, and in our case, the missing engine is a very deep set of specialized Google AdWords expertise that allows the money to be spent.

Without the engine, your Cadillac won't run; without specialized AdWords expertise, neither will your Ad Grant.

This very specialized expertise is something most nonprofits simply don't have. And you shouldn't feel about about that, because even most digital marketing experts don't even have a lot of specialized Google AdWords expertise; it's a very niche job within an even-more-niche skill set.

Think about it for a second. If Google's been giving away $10,000 in monthly advertising to (almost) all comers for 13 years and most nonprofits still don't use it, there's gotta be a serious catch. Let's break down the catch – or, more accurately, catches – below.

Google doesn't give you real money. If Google were cutting checks for $10,000 cash every month and sending them to every nonprofit in the world, then obviously, every charity would be signed up and stampeding toward the Googleplex in Mountain View in the amount of time it's taken you to read this paragraph. Hell, you'd have people creating new nonprofits in droves, simply to get their hands on all that money. But that's not the case, and that part really is no big surprise. The program would be rife with fraud potential, not to mention the fact that Google is a profit-seeking enterprise, so handing out big monthly checks to millions of nonprofits around the world would make a considerable dent in its balance sheet.

No, your $10,000 a month in free advertising -- actually, $329 per day, but we'll cover that distinction later – comes in the form of an "unbilled account," which is basically Google's version of store credit. Sounds good, right? $10,000 a month in store credit with Google is still better than a sharp stick in the eye. You can just spend it on any kind of advertising you want, whenever and wherever you want, right?

Well, no. Not even close, actually. Google AdWords has a wide, wide array of advertising features and options: video ads, lightbox ads, animated display ads, non-animated display ads, display text ads, call-only phone ads, responsive ads and, of course, search ads, the little text ads that display as a result of what you search for on Google.com. And your Ad Grant allows you access to only one of them.

You must use your ad credit on search ads. With Google Ad Grants, you're allowed to use your $10,000 per month only on search ads. That means no display ads, no graphics, no logos and no video. No deciding what sites you'd like to run your ads on. No deciding what demographics or interest groups to target. An Ad Grants account is restricted to bidding only on keywords and to have your text-only ads appear in Google search engine results pages (known as SERPs) as a result of people searching for a keyword that you've "bid" on.

So once again, let's amend our analogy of the Google Ad Grant. It's not cash; it's store credit. But it's not carte-blanche store credit, where you can buy whatever the store sells; it's heavily restricted, you-can-pick-things-only-from-these-three-aisles store credit.

OK, then. It's restricted, but you can still pick anything you like from those three aisles, and once you decide what you want to spend your $10,000 on, you load it up into your "cart" and check out. Boom, you've got $10,000 of free advertising coming in. Right?

Well, no. (We know, we know. We're being a total downer.)

You have to figure out on your own what people are searching for. Here's the biggest of all the catches inherent in Google Ad Grants: Search advertising is tough. You can go out and bid on 500 keywords that you think are great, but if the rest of the world isn't actually typing those 500 keywords into Google and hitting "search," no one will ever even see your ads, let alone click on them. And in the cases where people *are* searching for the keywords you've chosen, you still have to compete for people's attention with all the ads from all the other advertisers whose ads are showing as a result of those same keyword searches.

But at least you've got $329 per day to spend, and you can use that $329 any way you like, namely by bidding aggressively on the keywords that produce the most results, right? Well ... (OK, you knew it was coming this time) no.

Your bids are severely restricted. Competing with the entire universe of both nonprofit and for-profit advertisers is tough, because with Ad Grants, the maximum you're allowed to bid on any single click from any particular keyword is $2. By comparison, cash-paying, for-profit advertisers can bid up to $100 a click. For the not-so-mathematically inclined: For-profit businesses have literally *50 times the bidding power* in their account that you have in your Ad Grants account. (Side note: If you're confused by all this keyword-bidding business and how it works, don't worry. We'll cover that later as well.)

So one last time, let's bring our Google Ad Grant analogy into focus for total accuracy. It's not cash; it's store credit. But you can spend the store credit only in three specific aisles of the store. And you can't load anything into your cart without first reading a 150-page manual on the specific ways that you're permitted to load things into your cart. And once you've read the manual and are ready to load up your cart ... you have to do it with your wrists duct-taped together.

Oh, and you have to do all this at the same time you're doing your regular, 50-hours-per-week job with your nonprofit.

Piece of cake, right?

So there you have the true picture of Google Ad Grants. Yes, it's a Cadillac, and yes, it's totally free. But just like the Caddy won't run without a well-oiled engine propelling it down the road, an Ad Grant won't propel your nonprofit skyward without a great deal of knowledge and expertise about how the AdWords system works and how to maximize performance.

This is why so few nonprofits take advantage of Ad Grants: It's just too damned hard to master when your primary vocation is not Google AdWords management. And turning yourself (or a staff member or a volunteer) into an AdWords whiz isn't usually feasible; it takes years to achieve AdWords mastery, even when you give it your undivided attention. And really, who has any undivided attention these days?

It's a tough row to hoe, and that's why millions of nonprofit organizations worldwide have simply taken a pass on Ad Grants.

But you don't have to.

This book will explore two options for bang-up success with Google Ad Grants: contracted management and self-management. Contracted management is the easy part and doesn't require much explanation; you pay experts a little money every month to manage all of it for you. Sure, we own an agency that specializes in Ad Grants management, and we'd obviously be delighted to have you as a customer, but we wrote this book to help those of you who may choose to go it alone. More power to you! This is the only step-by-step instruction manual you'll ever need.

In the next chapter, you'll learn all the essential features and concepts of Google AdWords you'll need to expertly manage an Ad Grants account. These include:

1. How to sign up for Google for Nonprofits, the parent/precursor program that houses Google Ad Grants.
2. The basic structure of an AdWords account and how to build one from scratch.
3. How to create ads and how to split-test (A/B test) them for maximum performance.
4. How to research, add and bid on keywords.
5. How to set your ad budgets.
6. How to target specific geographic areas with advertising.
7. How to schedule your ads to run at specific times of day.
8. How to submit your AdWords account to Google for approval and conversion into an Ad Grants account.

Let's dive in, shall we?

THE NONPROFIT GUIDE TO HACKING GOOGLE ADWORDS

(Or, "Everything You Need to Know About Google Advertising and Nothing You Don't")

Steven Tyler once said, "You gotta learn to crawl before you learn to walk." And if Aerosmith said it, it must be true; they couldn't keep filling arenas for 40 years if they were callous, unscrupulous liars, could they?

So before you understand Google Ad Grants, you have to understand Google AdWords, the flagship advertising program and revenue engine that transformed Google from bootstrapped garage project into the world's largest advertising company and, in our opinion, the most impactful company the world has ever known.

Google AdWords is a lot like Home Depot: There are seemingly a million sections, nooks and crannies full of varied product offerings, it's nearly impossible to find what you're looking for without help, and it's quite possible to get lost altogether. So that's why we've created this special section: It includes only what you need to know about Google AdWords as it relates to managing a Google Ad Grant, and we omit everything else. Guides on the whole AdWords system have been written many times (we recommend <u>Perry Marshall's Ultimate Guide to AdWords</u>, if you're so inclined). We're busy guys, and we know you're busy too, so you don't need us cranking out hundreds of pages on it.

What's Google AdWords, exactly? Here's how I explain it to newbies:

> *Me: You know how when you do a Google Search and you see the special links that come up that say "AD" on them, and they're related to what you just searched for?*
>
> *Newbie: Yes. Yes, I do.*
>
> *Me: That's Google AdWords.*

There you go; that's the five-second version of what Google AdWords is all about. It allows companies to show you ads based on whatever keywords you just typed into Google before hitting the Search button. In the tiniest fraction of a second between the moment you clicked "Search" and the moment your search results came up, Google figured out which of its millions of advertisers deserved to have their ad show front and center as a result of your query.

This instantaneous coupling of every user's search query with a closely related advertising message is the single greatest reason that Google is the world-dominating behemoth that it is today.

And there is no close second. Advertisers worldwide pay top dollar for the opportunity to get their message in front of you mere milliseconds after you have expressed a desire for one of their products or services via your search query. It's the essence of "striking while the iron is hot."

Every single one of the countless other pies Google has its fingers in – phones, computers, self-driving cars, maps, software, virtual reality, telecom, YouTube, payment systems, drones, space travel, etc. – was financed with AdWords money, money that came from users clicking on ads that popped up in the eye-blink of time following a Google search.

Impressive, eh?

So that's the foundation of what you need to know about Google AdWords. Users search for X, ads related to X appear, and users click on those ads.

Let's step back to our Ad Grants corner of the world, then. Google Ad Grants lets you harness this simple but world-changing AdWords power: the power to tell someone about your nonprofit at the very instant they've performed a search query that's related to what you do.

How do you do that? How do you take the reins of this enormously powerful system – a system that can get you in front of millions of people around the globe instantly – and get your message in front of the right people at the right time?

It's just like building a house: step by step, brick by brick. The seven basic steps you'll be learning here are:

1. Joining Google for Nonprofits
2. Creating an AdWords account
3. Creating a campaign
4. Creating an ad group
5. Creating ads
6. Adding keywords
7. Submitting your account for Ad Grants acceptance

This house isn't going to build itself, so let's attack those steps!

Note: We're writing this book in late 2016, and the instructions you see here are based on the way Google has its setup pages configured right this minute. And although Google is known to change up the look of its pages once in a while, you can rest assured that they'll always make the setup process very obvious and easy to follow. We'll update this book if the process ever changes so significantly that the forthcoming instructions are no longer helpful, but at least for now, they reflect Google's current signup process.

STEP ONE: JOIN GOOGLE FOR NONPROFITS

Google Ad Grants is just one of several services that Google provides for charities under the umbrella of its "Google for Non-profits" program (we, like the other cool kids, refer to it as GFN). To take advantage of Ad Grants, you first must sign up for GFN, and you do that here:

www.google.com/nonprofits/eligibility

The process takes about 10 or 15 minutes. Most of that time is consumed by the new-in-2016 requirement to validate your nonprofit with TechSoup.org, but even with that additional step, it's quick. Enter your nonprofit's vital information, and make sure you have your tax ID number handy. You can't apply for either GFN or TechSoup validation without it.

After these quick steps, you should be accepted into the program immediately, although in some cases, it takes up to 48 hours.

The next step may seem a little backwards, but for reasons known only to Google, it's designed it a little backwards. It goes like this:

1. Once you're accepted into GFN, you create an AdWords account, carefully following the very specific rules and restrictions of the Ad Grants program.
2. Then and only then can you apply for Google Ad Grants. You do this by submitting a short form with your account

number on it. It's like saying, "Hey, Google, here's the account I built for Ad Grants. Does it meet your approval?"
3. Then you're officially approved for Ad Grants, and you're rolling.

Now that we've explained Google's confusing process, on to the next step: creating your AdWords account.

STEP TWO: CREATE AN ADWORDS ACCOUNT

Saddle up to your computer and type in www.google.com/adwords. And definitely use your computer, not a phone or even a tablet. The AdWords system is still too complicated to tackle on anything but a computer.

One of the first things you'll see on the AdWords home page is a big green button that says "Start Now." Click that to get started.

On the following page, you're asked for your email and your website, but don't enter those. In the first paragraph, you'll see a link that says "Skip the Guided Setup." Click that. (Don't worry, we're your guides now. Who needs Google?)

On the following page, you'll be asked to enter four pieces of information: your email address, country, time zone and currency. You won't be able to change any of these later; then again, I can't imagine a case in which you'd need to (your nonprofit isn't moving to another country, your time zone isn't going to change, and neither is your currency). You're asked for your time zone so that, if you decide to schedule ads to run at a certain time, the times you choose will be reflected accurately. Choose the currency used by your home nation (even though you won't be spending any actual money, you still have to do this so Google knows how much advertising credit to give you each day).

Once you've submitted this data, Google may or may not ask you to enter a phone number for additional account security, and there's nothing at all wrong with giving yourself some additional account security. You will also be prompted to enter billing information. NEVER, EVER enter billing information. This account is a regular cash-paying account at this very moment, but later on, at the end of this process, we're going to have Google convert it into an unbilled Ad Grants account. So always skip the billing information part. I'll risk annoying you by repeating this one more time: NEVER ENTER BILLING INFORMATION. If you ever enter billing information into an AdWords account, you have to start all over again.

But after that, boom, you're done. You've created an AdWords account. Not too painful at all.

STEP THREE: CREATE A CAMPAIGN

The next thing for you to do is build a campaign. But what's a "campaign," exactly?

In AdWords, a campaign is a collection of ad groups (we'll get to those later) that share the same budget, targeting and distribution settings. It is the highest-level structural unit inside an AdWords account; every piece of advertising you do *must* start with a campaign. Among the targeting methods determined at the campaign level are the users' physical location, the type of device they're using and the language they speak.

You can create as many campaigns in your AdWords account as you like, targeting as many swathes of people as you like (Technically, there's a hard limit of 10,000 campaigns that can be deployed in an AdWords account, but since you're a nonprofit and have only $329 a day to spend, you're in no danger of hitting that ceiling).

For example, you may have a nonprofit that serves people nationwide, and thus you may want a campaign to show ads to the entire United States.

But then you also may have a specific fundraising event in Colorado that you want to advertise only to those people who are likely to be able to attend that fundraiser – i.e., people in or near Colorado. In that case, you'd need to build a separate campaign for that particular fundraiser, targeting only the geographic areas that you believe would be beneficial. Because the geographic targeting is set at the campaign level, you must create separate campaigns if you want to show certain ads only to people in certain geographic areas.

This process can be repeated for as many geographic areas for which you may want to advertise.

When you start an account, you'll be prompted to create your first campaign with a big ol' button that says, appropriately enough, "Create Your First Campaign," so you can click that to get started.

On the following screen, you'll give your campaign a name. You can call it whatever you like, but for our purposes here, you're welcome to accept the default name, which is "Campaign #1."

The "Campaign Type" dropdown menu will give you the option of several types of campaigns. "Search Network Only" is the only correct option for Google Ad Grants; all others will put you in violation of the Ad Grants terms and conditions (you cannot do display, shopping, app or video advertising with Grants).

Once you've chosen "Search Network Only," there's a little set of radio buttons to the right for you to choose from. Choose "All Features" instead of the checked-by-default "Standard" option. Leave the other bubbles in this section unchecked, including the bubbles about mobile apps, dynamic search ads, etc.

Next, you'll move on to "Networks," where Google search and search partners will be checked by default. You MUST uncheck the box that says "include search partners"; you're not allowed to check this box with Ad Grants.

Next up, "Locations." Remember that every ad, ad group, etc. will show in every location chosen at this level, so choose your geo target accordingly. You can always edit this later, but you want to set it up correctly the first time, as you will have many things to juggle once the campaign goes live. If you're a nationwide charity, choose the whole country. If you're more local, choose the regions, states and/or cities that are most appropriate. On the other hand, if you're an international charity, choose the whole world (known in Google settings as "All countries & territories")!

You can get even more granular if you'd like, typing in a city or cities that you want to target. You may also click on "advanced search" and target by radius around a certain city or ZIP code, or even a particular street address. There are a lot of ways to set up geotargeting, and it's very easy to change these settings at any time, so don't worry about getting it perfect the first time around. If you're in doubt, select your home state, and let's move forward.

You'll also see a little link called "Location Options (Advanced)." Click the plus sign to untwist your options, because there's a very important change you need to make in this section. Your default selection is going to say "People in, or who show interest in my targeted location (recommended.)" Despite Google's "recommendation," you don't want this bubble checked. Change it to "People in my targeted location," period.

Here's the reason: Google is extremely fast and loose with whom it considers to "show interest in my target location." Let's say you want to advertise only to people in the United States, which is not uncommon. If you leave your settings on Google's recommended bubble, you'll get clicks on your ads from people all over the world – people you thought you were specifically excluding when you made your country selection – simply because those people, at some point in the recent past, performed a Google search that had something, anything, to do with the good old U. S. of A.

Here's a timely example: People all over the world were watching the results of the 2016 US presidential election more closely than any other time since the Internet was invented. Millions of people outside the US were Googling our election results. And guess what? Now, all of those millions of people are considered by Google to have "shown interest in your target location." And if it weren't for this little paragraph teaching you how to uncheck that little bubble, those millions would be among those seeing and clicking your ad. You're welcome!

OK, onward. Next, select your language. If you're reading this, it's most likely English, but just to be clear: What you're selecting here is the language spoken by the people you'd like to have see your ads. You may choose multiple languages – or all languages, for that matter – but be aware that in an overwhelming majority of cases, the language you select should match the language in which your ads and website are written. So choose accordingly.

Your bid strategy will be the next selection, and for this you must select "Manual CPC" (cost per click), which should be the default selection. There will be a box to the right which will be automatically checked that says "Use Enhanced CPC." BE SURE TO UNCHECK THIS BOX. You're not allowed to use Enhanced CPC with an Ad Grants account.

Your default per-click bid is next, and this should be set to $2. This bid tells Google, "I'm willing to spend $2 of my daily advertising credit anytime someone clicks on my ad." Two dollars is the maximum bid allowed within the Grants program. You can never, ever, under any circumstances set your bid higher than $2; if you do, you'll be violating the terms of service, and your account can be permanently suspended. And although there are occasional instances in which a bid lower than $2 makes sense (we'll talk about that later), the overwhelming majority of the time, you'll want this bid set at the full $2 you're allowed. Google advertising is very competitive, and you'll want to bid as aggressively as you're allowed to.

Your next setting is Budget, which should be set at $329 per day. This assumes that all of the advertising you'll be doing in your entire Ad Grants account will be spent from this specific campaign. That may not be the case for very long, and we'll show you later on how to set up a shared budget so that your $329 can be, well, shared across several campaigns. But for now, since this is your first campaign, give it the full $329.

The next step will be to choose "Delivery Method." By default, this will be set to "Standard," which means Google will ration the display of your ads evenly throughout all 24 hours of the day so that you don't run out of budget before midnight. You might think this is good – especially since it's Google's "recommended" setting – but we're contrarians, and we don't like it. We advise you switch it to "Accelerated." Here's why.

When Standard delivery is enabled, Google's going to let you spend only about $13 or $14 per hour of your $329 allotment. After all, if you spend any more than that per hour, you'll run out of money before midnight, and that's the point of Standard delivery: to let your ads run at all hours. But what that means in practice is that Google simply stops your ads from showing on hundreds, maybe thousands, of relevant keyword searches earlier in the day so that you've still got some budget left over to show the night owls when they're searching for those same relevant keywords as midnight draws near.

Is that smart? Is it a good strategy? Well, maybe – but maybe not. If I'm managing your nonprofit's Ad Grants account and Google tells me that it's not going to show my ad to someone at 9:30 a.m. because it wants to save the budget so it can show ads to someone else at 10 p.m., my response is simply: Why? Why is that a good thing? Does Google have data showing me that nighttime visitors are more likely to donate money to my organization or sign up for my e-mail newsletter or buy a ticket to my next fundraiser than people who click my ads in the daytime? No, it absolutely does not have data like that. So why are we taking a pass on daytime visitors – visitors who, again, are actively searching for what my nonprofit has to offer – in favor of the night-timers?

Google's answer goes something like this: "Well, unless you run ads during all 24 hours of the day, then you'll never know which hours draw the most productive visitors." And that's true … but in our opinion, that's not a strong enough argument to take a pass on a significant amount of workday ad impressions.

Instead, I want to run full-on, unrestricted traffic; I want to run my entire campaign up the Internet flagpole and see who salutes, without Google's opaque algorithm refusing to show my ads on a majority of my daytime traffic. If I do that and the Internet hordes gobble up all my daily allotted ad clicks by 4 a.m. and they don't take any meaningful action, no problem. I can adjust my ad scheduling and try some other times of day. But until then, I want to test my ads against all of Google's traffic with no restrictions, and that's why we recommend Accelerated delivery.

Now, let's skip down the page to "Ad Delivery: Ad Rotation, Frequency Capping." Again, we're going to rebel against Google's recommended setting of "Optimize for clicks" and instead choose "rotate indefinitely." But why wouldn't you want to optimize for clicks? After all, that's what we want, right? Clicks, visits to our website? Yes, we do.

But here's where we have to take a longer view than Google does. Google's algorithm – in our humble opinion – makes its decisions far too quickly about which of your ads will generate more clicks over the long haul. This is a beef we've had with Google for many years, and make no mistake, it's a contrarian view. But we've seen countless cases in which Google picks a "winning" ad early on and stops delivering other, possibly better ads without giving the new ones a chance to compete against its chosen champion. We'll talk more about this later, but constantly testing new ad copy approaches is key to your success with AdWords, and the recommended setting here short-circuits that process of continuous ad improvement.

By contrast, the "rotate indefinitely" setting lets you choose when low-performing ads get turned off. The process of testing ads against one another is called "A/B testing" or "split-testing" (we prefer the latter term), and it's critical to do that correctly, and with a watchful eye on the statistical significance of your ad performance. But we'll talk more about that later. For now, just check "rotate indefinitely," and we'll come back to this topic a bit later on.

Finally, untwist the "Schedule" plus sign. Although for most campaigns, the best approach is to run your ads 24/7, there can be occasions why it may be better to run the ads on a set schedule. Say your advertising is encouraging people to make a phone call to your nonprofit, but you have no one to take those calls on nights or weekends. In that case, you may not want to run ads during those times where no one can answer the phones.

Or maybe you've been running your ads for a while and have studied a significant amount of data, only to find that there are certain times of day when your ads just don't perform well at all. You may want to shut your ads off during those down times (Be sure that you have plenty of data to back this up before you make such a change; a couple of weeks' worth of data may not represent what will happen in the long run).

It's possible to schedule your ads to be on or off at any time of day or any day of the week. To do this, go to the settings tab within a campaign, click the "edit" button next to "Ad Scheduling," click "Create Custom Schedule" and set the days and times you'd like your campaign to run. Voila.

For now, the rest of the settings on this page can be left as-is.

A note on budget sharing

As mentioned many times earlier, the maximum amount you are allowed to spend per day in your Ad Grants account is $329, and that's true whether you have one campaign or 100. If you have multiple campaigns, one way to ensure that you stay under the limit is to split that $329 up into separate budgets for each campaign. As long as the grand total of those budgets is $329, you're fine.

But that's the hard way. The easy way is to create a "shared budget," which is one $329-per-day budget that will cover all of the campaigns in your account. This will dole out the full budget indiscriminately, on a first-come, first-served basis. So maybe each of your campaigns will get a roughly equal amount of budget spent, or it may be that one campaign gets the lion's share. However, using the shared budget method, you don't have to manually assign specific chunks of money to each campaign and do scratch-paper math in order to add them all up to $329.

The way to set up a shared budget is to navigate to any page in your account and look at the left sidebar (if you do not see a sidebar area, click the double-arrow chevron at the top left of the page under the Google AdWords logo, which will reveal the sidebar). Toward the bottom, click on the link that says "Shared Library."

Once you are in the Shared Library, you'll have several options, one of which is "Budgets." Click on Budgets and then, on the next page, click the red "+Budget" button. This is where you will create your shared budget.

First, it will ask you to name your budget. Something like "All Campaigns Shared Budget" is fine. No one will see this but you, so you can call it anything you like.

Then, you'll be asked to select the campaigns to which you'd like to apply this budget. In other words, Google's saying, "Tell us which campaigns that you'd like to have sharing this $329 budget." Since we're talking about one budget to share for all campaigns, in this area, you should add all of the active campaigns to that budget by clicking the edit link and moving your applicable campaigns from the left-side box to the right-side box.

Once you have moved all of the campaigns you want into the right-side box, move down to the next step and enter the budget amount, which in this case should be the entire $329. Then save it.

Now, if you navigate back to your campaigns page (via the Campaigns link at the top of any page), you should see that all of your active campaigns have a budget called "All Campaigns Shared Budget," and it should reflect a $329-per-day budget. All of the columns should look the same. If any campaigns do not reflect this, go back to the Shared Library to be sure that all of the active campaigns have been added to that budget.

Always be sure that, at the bottom left corner of your

Campaigns page in the gray area of the "Budget" column, the grand total budget is $329. If there is any number higher than $329 in that spot, you haven't set it up correctly. In essence, you're telling Google to spend more than your allotted $329, and that violates your terms of service.

STEP FOUR: CREATE AD GROUPS

Congrats! You've got an AdWords account set up, and you've got one campaign all tuned up and ready to go. What do you do next? You create some "ad groups."

Ad groups are housed inside campaigns and are made up of two basic elements: ads, and the keywords that trigger those ads to appear atop Google search results when a user types in one of the keywords that we've chosen to bid on.

Here's your easy-peasy example of how keywords and ads work together within an ad group: Let's say our charity is the Boys Club of Rapid City, and the Boys Club would like to solicit donations to its Christmas gift program, wherein generous local folks pick a card off a Christmas tree, open it, see that there's a needy boy named Tommy who wants a warm coat for Christmas, buy the coat, deliver it to the Boys Club, etc. We know there are people who search Google for these types of programs during the holidays, and maybe they type things like "Christmas donations" or "Rapid City gift trees." So we will bid on those keywords: "Christmas donations" and "Rapid City gift trees."

POP QUIZ! How much will we bid? That's right, $2. We'll put our maximum bid of $2 on those keywords. And so, when people type "Christmas donations" or "Rapid City gift trees" into Google, our ad will appear at the top of the search results. It'll say "Make A Christmas Dream Come True For An Underprivileged Boy At The Rapid City Boys Club" or something like that.

That's how the keywords and ads work together in an ad group: You select the keywords you want to bid on (e.g., "Christmas donations"), and then you create an ad that's displayed front and center (e.g. "Make A Christmas Dream Come True…") when someone searches for one of your keywords. Easy, right?

Each ad group should contain a small batch of keywords (about 10 to 15 keywords) with a small batch of corresponding ads (usually about two to three ads per ad group). Each ad group should revolve around a common theme, which is the reason for including so few keywords in each ad group.

Why, exactly, should our ad groups each revolve around one narrow theme? It's because Google gives great weight to ad relevance, specifically "keyword-to-ad relevance." Sounds complicated, but it's basically this: Does your ad text match up well, or accurately reflect, your keywords? For instance, does your keyword appear in the ad text itself? How about in the headline? Google likes that even more. So the more closely your ads resemble and reflect the keywords tied to that ad, the better.

Now, Google ads are pretty short. We'll get to the specifics of exactly how short in a little bit, but you know they're short, because you've seen the ads when doing Google searches of your own. So how many keywords could you possibly have in an ad group that also match up well with the ad text? That's right, not very many. Only a handful of keywords are going to be close enough in meaning that they match up well with the text of one small ad. Thus, to keep all of your ads relevant, you keep the number of keywords in any particular ad group very small. Like, 10 to 15, tops.

Let's say I have a nonprofit that helps pay the utility bills for families of people who are battling cancer. I might make one ad group only for the keywords "cancer charity" and "cancer charities," and I'd be sure to use those phrases in my ad text. Then, I might make a second ad group for the keywords "local charity" and "local charities," and in that ad group, I'd make sure my ads used *those* words in my ad text. Then maybe one for "cancer nonprofit(s)," another for "cancer victims" and so on. Always small, closely related chunks of a dozen or so keywords, with those keywords reflected in my ad text.

Setting up an ad group is as simple as navigating to the ad group tab within your campaign and clicking the red "+ AD GROUP" button. You'll be asked to name the ad group. Choose a name that fits the tightly knit bundle of keywords you will choose, so it can be easily identifiable when you're studying the data later on.

You'll then be asked to tackle the last two steps of the process: creating an ad and adding some keywords.

STEP FIVE: CREATE AN AD

To create your first ad, choose the "text ad" radio button at the top of the page (this should be the default choice), because text ads are the only type of ads allowed in Google Ad Grants. Then, fill in the blank fields.

First is the "Final URL" field. This is the page on your site you want the person to land on when they click your ad. Often, people just put the home page of their site, and often, that is just fine.

However, if your ad group is focusing on a certain event, fundraiser, feature, etc., and you have a page on your site dedicated to that event, fundraiser or feature, it's best to send them to that page. The more a person has to navigate the site to find exactly what they searched for, the more of a chance they will leave the site, never to return.

Next are the lines of ad text, the advertisement that Google searchers will actually see. With a text ad, you are allowed to have two headlines of 30 characters each (spaces count) and one description area that consists of up to 80 characters (again, spaces count). The field labeled "path" is an advanced tracking feature that will not be used for our purposes in this book.

There are a couple of restrictions here. You're not allowed to use an exclamation point in the headline(s) and not more than one in the body of the ad. You also may not use symbols (*please donate*) or excessive capitalization (PLEASE DONATE). Don't worry too much about memorizing these rules; AdWords will alert you if you run afoul of them, and your ad will not be approved. The full list of editorial rules can be found here:

https://support.google.com/adwordspolicy/answer/6021546

Anyone can write an ad, of course, but it takes creativity, data collection and a lot of testing to write good ads. Ultimately, it will be the people searching who will tell you if your ad is good or not (by way of clicks, clickthrough rates and conversions), but you can give yourself a leg up by starting out in a better position than just throwing a bunch of you-know-what at the wall to see what sticks.

First, you'll want to make sure that the keywords in that particular ad group also appear in the ad. Using our example of "local charity," we would want to be sure that our ads contain that particular phrase.

The reason for this is that people are generally more likely to click on an ad when they see their exact search term within the text of that ad. Also, Google really likes it when your keywords, ad text and landing pages all line up nicely, and it rewards you by bestowing better "Quality Scores" upon your keywords. We won't go into the gory details of Quality Scores here; suffice it to say that better Quality Scores lead to cheaper click costs.

Though it may seem silly to care about cost per click since, technically, you aren't paying for the clicks, it does make a big difference. The cheaper your clicks, the more people you get to your website each day from your $329 allotment.

There is a trick of the trade you can use to get this result without having to spell out the keywords in every single ad you write, and that trick is called Dynamic Keyword Insertion (or DKI). DKI is an automated function that will automatically insert the exact text typed by the user straight into the ad text itself.

For example, in my "local charity" ad group, someone can type in "local charity" and see my ad, but they could also type in "charity in my area" to see it. If I am using DKI in the headline of my ad, the headline the person sees will be exactly what they typed in. In this case, "Local Charity" for the first example and "Charity In My Area" for the next.

You're essentially telling Google, "Hey, whatever the user types in – just make that my headline." And Google says, "10-4, good buddy, will do." (You can also use DKI in the description of your ad, but that's tough. It can lead to some pretty nonsensical-sounding ads if you're not careful.)

So, here's a quandary. We know our headline has a max capacity of 30 characters. So what if you're using a DKI headline and the user happens to input a phrase longer than 30 characters? Something like "I Want to Donate to a Local Charity"?

No worries. The DKI syntax contains a default headline specifically for this purpose. If the user's query is too long, Google swaps out your default text, and you're good to go.

DKI is easy to implement. Simply insert this into your ad box ...

{KeyWord:Default Ad Text}

… wherever you want to use DKI. And replace "Default Ad Text" with whatever generic text you'd like to have appear if the user's query is too long. You'll get the most mileage out of this by placing this text in the "Headline 1" section of your ad.

Here's an example of a DKI ad:

{KeyWord:Support A Local Charity} – Donate To Coats For Kids ATL.
Help A Local Kid Keep Warm This Winter. Please Donate Now. Any Amount Helps!

What does the user see in this scenario?

1. If the user searches for "Christmas donation tree" – which is fewer than 30 characters – he or she will see this:

    Christmas Donation Tree – Donate To Coats For Kids ATL.
    Help A Local Kid Keep Warm This Winter. Please Donate Now. Any Amount Helps!

    Note that Google sucks the user query right into your ad and makes it your headline. Nice!

2. If the user searches for "Christmas volunteering

opportunities in Atlanta" – which is way, way longer than 30 characters – he or she will see this:

Support A Local Charity – Donate To Coats For Kids ATL. Help A Local Kid Keep Warm This Winter. Please Donate Now. Any Amount Helps!

In this case, Google notices that the search phrase is too long to be used for its headline, and it uses your default headline. Also nice!

Warning! Everything from the brackets to the spacing to the capitalization in the DKI code is important. The braces are necessary, and you cannot use DKI without them. The capitalization of the K and W in "KeyWord" is also necessary; it ensures that your headline is rendered in title casing (i.e. Every Word Is Capitalized, Like This), which has been demonstrated to increase clickthrough rate. Finally, the space, or lack thereof, after the colon is also important in that it allows you to get the maximum allowable characters into your headline.

Beyond these technical-ish matters, you should also remember that writing an ad is your time to be creative. Think outside the box. Have fun. Say interesting stuff. Be funny. Be conversational. This isn't an ad copywriting book, because that'd be another full-length project entirely. But the one piece of advice we give to aspiring AdWords copywriters is this: Write your Google ads like you're talking to a good friend. Don't be loud and garish. Speak naturally and with familiarity. Most Google ads are badly written, and they scream at the user instead of initiating a conversation *with* the user. The second way works far, far better.

You can have fun with it and make good ads as well. After all, we never know whether our ad is good or will fall flat until we put it out there, let it run for a while and then split-test it against the other ads in the same ad group.

What's "split-testing," you ask?

Split-testing, also known as A/B testing, is the ongoing process of running two or more ads at the same time to see which one performs better. In every ad group, you should always be running at least two ads simultaneously. This is how you continuously improve your results over the long haul.

Sure, you can write one ad and call it good, but one thing's for sure: Unless you're the greatest copywriter the world has ever known, you probably didn't write the best-producing, results-driving ad that your account will ever see on your first crack. No one does. You've just begun the process of showing your message to your audience. Who knows what ad text will yield the best response? It can't be known until you test multiple sets of ad copy.

So write two ads for each group. Say different things, or the same thing in different ways, or do both. Every month or so, come back and look at the performance differences between your ads. Is there an ad that's clearly performing worse than the other, with a markedly lower clickthrough rate? Pause it – it's now officially the "loser" – and write another one to compete against your "champion" ad that won the first split-test. Lather, rinse, repeat – forever!

We mean that: forever. Unless you've been faithfully split-testing every ad group each month or so for many years, it's unlikely that you've tried every ad copy approach available to you. Keep writing ads that challenge your reigning "champion" ad, the ad that's produced the best result. This will lead to higher and higher clickthrough rates, which will make your clicks cheaper and cheaper, which means your $329 will buy you more and more website visitors over time.

Once your ads are in place and your URLs are pointing to the right page of your site, you can move to the next section, which is adding keywords.

STEP SIX: ADD KEYWORDS

Let's take a closer look at keywords, because they are the lifeblood of Google AdWords, which is a pay-per-click system. Every time someone clicks on one of your ads, you pay. You, of course, are paying with house money, but you pay all the same.

But how much do you pay for each click? That's where keywords come in.

Everything starts with keywords, because when a user types keywords into a Google search bar, that's what gets the ball rolling.

Keywords are where the users first express their intent.

Every keyword you include in your account must have a bid associated with it. Your bids, in an Ad Grant, will almost always be set at $2 per click (because that's the maximum allowable bid). That simply means you're telling Google the following:

"When someone searches for 'nonprofit volunteer opportunities,' I'm willing to pay $2 for that person to click my ad. So please consider that, Almighty Google, as you decide which ads to show the thousands of people searching for 'nonprofit volunteer opportunities' each month. If you show my ad and the user clicks it, there's two crisp George Washingtons in it for you."

And Google says, "OK, thank for your bid. We'll take your offer under consideration every time someone searches for 'nonprofit volunteer opportunities,' and we'll get back to you. Don't call us, we'll call you."

That's keyword bidding in a nutshell. You make your strongest offer – which in your case is $2 per click – and Google decides whether that offer is attractive enough to show your ads to its users. Pretty simple.

Let's reiterate that the maximum allowable bid is $2, so never bid more on any keyword. You don't want to get kicked out of the program!

OK, you get it. So about the keywords themselves. How do you go about choosing what keywords are right for your nonprofit?

Well, the first step is always just to think about it logically. We start with the most general keywords and work our way toward more specific keywords. If we look at our nonprofit in general terms – and I mean the most general terms you can think of – what do we see?

Let's say our nonprofit is a charity in Atlanta that helps buy winter coats for children in low-income families. From the most general standpoint, you would naturally choose keywords like local charity, local nonprofit, Atlanta charity, Georgia nonprofit, children's charity, etc. These are all very general, for people looking for any type of charity in your area.

Then, you can think in more specific terms. Whom is it that my charity benefits? Keywords like "nonprofits for children," "ATL child charities," "help kids in atlanta," "donate to georgia kids," "charity for winter coats" and "help poor children" all come to mind. People wanting to help out in more specific ways, or help more specific groups of people, will be using search terms such as these.

Next, you can think even more specifically. Are you having a fundraiser? Your Ad Grant is a great place to get the word out.

Let's say we're having a 5K run to raise money for these children who need winter coats. First, we can advertise for 5Ks in general, as there are people who like to run in these events no matter the cause. So "Atlanta 5K," "ATL 5K run" and "Georgia road races" would all be good choices.

Then, we can appeal to people who are interested specifically in charitable runs by selecting "charity 5K," "charity run" and "Atlanta charity race."

So now we've thought of a handful of keyword and ad group ideas, but we get stuck on that handful and can't think of any more. How do you research for new keyword ideas?

Many times, it's as simple as a Google search. We've often Googled "keyword ideas for a (insert cause here: hunger, AIDS, cancer, etc.) nonprofit" and gotten many good keyword ideas.

It's also always a good idea to look over all of your website pages for ideas. Many of the keywords you will want to use are right there in your website copy.

After you've exhausted those possibilities, you can navigate your way to the single best keyword tool there is in all the universe – and you won't have to look far. In fact, it's snugly nestled right inside AdWords itself, although it's extremely well-hidden. In fact, it doesn't even have a name.

But here's how you find it.

As you know, both ads and keywords "live" inside an ad group. Once you've created an ad group that has at least a handful of keywords in it already, here's what we want you to do:

1. Navigate to your list of ad groups by clicking the "Campaigns" tab and then clicking on the name of the campaign that holds the ad group to which you'd like to add some keywords.

2. Find the ad group and click on its name.

3. On the next screen, click the "Keywords" tab.

4. On the following screen, there's a big red button that says "+KEYWORDS." Click that.

5. A beautiful thing happens. Two boxes appear. One is blank, and that's the one you can type keywords into if you like. But that's not why we're here.

6. Look at the other box on the right. It's smaller, but it's precious. It's inestimable. And as you can see, it is chock full of hundreds – possibly thousands – of keywords that are extremely similar to those on your list.

7. Not only that, they're already organized into themes. And they have beautiful – oh, so beautiful – little arrows next to them. All you have to do is click the little arrow, and all the keywords magically go right into the previously empty box on the left side.

8. You just look at them, adore them and click, click, click away. Add, add, add them to your left-side box. Add them until all the relevant keywords are out of the suggestion box and into your lovely left side box, and then click "save."

9. Weep a tear of joy for the insane number of work hours that Google's supremely intelligent servers have just saved you.

I get it. I can feel you judging my breathlessness over this tool, thinking I'm a little off my rocker. But just wait until you experience it for the first time. It's divine!

And in a matter of minutes, with only some mouse clicks, your ad groups are packed with relevant keywords. After adding them, you'll want to break these keywords up into new ad groups of 10 to 15 each, but for now, you've hit the jackpot on a new load of relevant terms.

Note: Do NOT confuse the process above with a much more prominently placed tool inside AdWords called "Keyword Planner." The Keyword Planner is a fine tool, but we don't find it well-suited to Ad Grants accounts, especially not for AdWords newbies. It's more useful for business accounts and requires quite an array of steps that are very complicated for the AdWords beginner. For our purposes, then, ignore the Keyword Planner tool.

So you've got a shiny new list of keywords, and that's fantastic. But there's one more step before you plug them into your newly created ad groups, and that is to include all the different match types for each keyword.

What are match types? Match types tell Google exactly how spot-on the user's query needs to be in order to show them your ads.

There are four match types for keywords, and they are – ranging from broadest to most restrictive – broad match, modified broad match, phrase match and exact match.

The more restrictive match types use special punctuation to demarcate them (more on that in a moment), but broad match keywords are just plain old words and phrases. If you type or paste a keyword into your ad group, by default, it will be a broad match keyword.

Broad match keywords look like this:

- Local charities
- Nonprofits
- Donate to charity

Broad match keywords allow your ad to be shown – well, quite broadly. Let's use the broad match keyword "local charity" as an example. You might be inclined to think, because you're bidding on this keyword, that only people who type "local charity" into Google will see your ad.

But believe you me – that ain't so.

When using broad match keywords, Google will show your ad not only to people who type in "local charity" but also to people who type in – and this is the official Google documentation talking here:

"relevant variations of your keywords, including synonyms, singular and plural forms, possible misspellings, stemmings (such as floor and

flooring), related searches and other relevant variations. This match type may also take the customer's recent search activities into account."

The first part sounds OK. Relevant variations are, well, relevant. Singulars, plurals, etc. But the parts about synonyms, related searches and your recent search activities? That's a VERY broad expansion of what the user can type into the search bar and trigger your ads.

We like to summarize it like this: With broad match keywords, Google will show ads not only to people who type those keywords but also to people who type anything Google's big scary artificially intelligent machine brain thinks is in any way similar to those keywords.

So if you're bidding on "local charity" as a broad match keyword, Google may also show your ad to people searching for any and all of the following searches:

- animal charities
- charity case
- charity stripe (i.e., the free-throw line in basketball)
- fraudulent charities
- Famous people named Charity
- Local schools

And so on.

This match type can bring in a lot of good traffic, but it can also cause lots of "waste," i.e., clicks from people who searched for something completely unrelated to your organization. So broad-match keywords should be managed very closely with negative keywords (more on that at the end of the section).

The next match type is the modified broad match (also referred to as broad match modified or expanded broad match). These are created by adding plus signs before each word of the keyword.

Modified broad match keywords look like this:

- +Local +charities
- +Nonprofits
- +Donate +to +charity

With modified broad match keywords, every individual word with a plus sign in front of it must be present in the user's search query for our ad to be triggered. It doesn't matter what other words the user includes, and it doesn't matter what order the user types them in, but the plus sign we stick behind each word requires that the user type that word in order for our ad to show up.

Naturally, this limits the power of Google's big-data-crunching mind to show our ads for what it considers "related" searches. With a broad match keyword of "donate to charity," Google could determine that Joe Schmoe's search for "charity scams" is similar enough to "donate to charity" that our ads should be displayed as a result of his scam search. But our plus signs are powerful. They overrule Google's big brain. Thus, if we have the modified broad match keyword of "+donate +to +charity" then Joe Schmoe's scam search won't trigger our ad. Why? Because it didn't contain the word "donate," the word "to" and the word "charity."

Next in the pecking order of restrictive match types is the phrase match keyword, which is denoted with quotation marks around the keyword.

Phrase match keywords look like this:

- "Local charities"
- "Nonprofits"
- "Donate to charity"

With this match type, not only must all of the words be present, they must be in the correct order as well. That's why it's called "phrase match": The entire phrase, exactly as typed by us in our phrase match keyword, must appear in the user's query. Otherwise, our ads won't be triggered.

So if this time around, Joe Schmoe searches for "find me a local charity," our ads would not be triggered. Why? Because "find me a local charity" does not contain the phrase "donate to charity" or "local charities." It's close, but close doesn't count with phrase match.

But what if Joe Schmoe types in "donate to charity in Atlanta" or "I want to donate to charity"? Yes, our ads would be triggered, because both of his queries contain our entire phrase, which is "donate to charity."

Finally, the most restrictive type is the exact match type, which is denoted by brackets around the keyword.

Exact match keywords look like this:

- [Local charities]
- [Nonprofits]
- [Donate to charity]

Exact match keywords are the easiest to explain. With these, the only way our ad's going to appear is if the user types in our keyword exactly, word for word, space for space, zero variations, zip, zilch, nada (other than capitalization; Google makes no distinction between uppercase and lowercase letters). Otherwise, our ads don't show.

So which of these match types should you include in your Ad Grants account? All of 'em.

Clearly, the exact match and phrase match searchers are more relevant. The guy who types in "donate to charity" and the lady who types in "charity volunteering opportunities" are the most interested, warm leads you're going to find. We know this. But everyone else knows it too, and thus, those are very competitive keywords. It's unlikely we'll appear in the search results much of the time for those. In an ideal world, we'd love to have our Ad Grants account firing off $329 worth of advertising based solely on those super-specific, super-warm leads.

But that ain't gonna happen. It's too competitive out there. So to cover all of your bases, just add all four match types for each keywords. That's the easy route to hoovering up as much relevant traffic as your $10,000 a month can buy.

But remember our regular old broad match keywords, the ones that can draw stinky, unrelated searches into our nice clean space here? How do we get the benefit of all that extra good traffic they can bring us, without all the garbage?

With negative keywords.

Negative keywords are your bonus fifth match type, although they behave quite differently from the other four. Negative keywords are the Google AdWords version of when your local watering hole or bodega or Chinese restaurant takes bad checks and sticks them in a little corkboard above the cash register with a big shaming sign that says "DO NOT ACCEPT CHECKS FROM THESE PEOPLE."

Except we do it with negative keywords, which are denoted with minus signs.

Negative keywords look like this:

- -fraudulent
- -bangs
- -jade

Why bangs and jade? Charity Jade and Charity Bangs are adult film stars, and lots of internet-folk search for them every day. And if you don't add their last names as negative keywords, your ads will be front and center whenever they do. Probably not the branding experience you're looking for.

So negative keywords are our own little personal corkboard above the cash register. And our corkboard says, "DO NOT SHOW OUR ADS IF ANY OF THESE WORDS ARE PRESENT IN A USER'S SEARCH."

Easy-peasy. Adios, porn starlets, and adios to any other unrelated terms that we don't want to waste on budget on.

Note: Please do not burden yourself with the soul-eating task of manually placing plus signs, quotation marks and brackets around thousands of individual keywords. Not only will you rocket yourself into the advanced stages of carpal tunnel syndrome far before your time, you'll also die of boredom at least once or twice, and after the first time, the emergency defibrillator in your office may not have been replaced yet. Instead, please continue reading the book. In a later chapter, we'll point you to a web tool that allows you to create all four match types for thousands of keywords with one click of the mouse. Tell your mouse hand we said you're welcome.

STEP SEVEN: SUBMIT YOUR ACCOUNT TO GOOGLE TO RECEIVE AD GRANTS STATUS

If you're sitting there thinking, "This is weird, and it can't be right, that I have to build an entire AdWords account BEFORE I even apply to the Ad Grants program to begin with? That's gotta be backward," I don't blame you. It's very backward, but I assure you, it's definitely right. Google's quirky and odd sometimes, and you just roll with the punches early to get to the holy grail.

Once you've finished all of the above steps, make a note of the account number at the top right corner of your AdWords screen (it's 10 digits and broken up with hyphens, just like a phone number). Then cruise back over to your GFN account and log in. You'll see a blue button that asks you to "Sign Up Now" for GFN services. Click it, and on the next page you'll see the Google Ad Grants program with another blue button that says "Enroll." Submit your account number there, check some boxes, and hit submit.

Then, go find something fun to do for the next week or so, because Google, in its massive September 2016 overhaul of the program, extended its approval period from 48 hours to 10 BUSI-NESS DAYS! Ouch! During that 10-day period, you'll get an email from Google asking you to verify that it was you, and not some impostor trying to hijack your organization, who signed up for Ad Grants. Tell 'em yes, wait a few more days, and bang – here comes a "welcome to the program!" email.

And you're officially off to the races.

So let's recap. You've joined GFN, created an AdWords account and created a campaign inside that account. Inside that campaign, you've got an ad group, and inside that ad group, you've added an array of keywords (with multiple match types, of course) and at least two ads that those keywords trigger. You've then gone over to your Google for Nonprofits account and submitted your AdWords account number to the team, and you've received a welcome letter back from the Big G that says, "Nice work, mate; you're in the club."

Congratulations, my friend, you're now advertising on Google! (We'd put a GIF here of a guy rabidly fist pumping or spraying champagne all over the place, but unfortunately, Amazon doesn't support that yet).

Now, the real work begins: You go back and repeat this process for each ad group, as many times as necessary, to create tons of ad groups, all containing small, tightly themed groups of keywords.

It's a big job, but we believe in you.

But wait. Now you know how to build your AdWords account. But what the heck should you actually put in it?

Get ready to limber up, friends. The answer is in the next chapter.

HOW TO LIMBER UP

(Or, "The Most Intelligent Ways to Use Your Google Ad Grant, Complete With Catchy Acronym!")

The day you get that lovely acceptance email from Google telling you there's a fresh $329 of ad money waiting for you today and every subsequent day until an asteroid hits the Earth, you might be hit with one overwhelming thought:

"What now?"

In other words, what the heck are we going to do with this money? What are we going to promote? What are we allowed to promote? What's the smartest way to spend it?

That's natural. After all, when's the last time somebody dropped an essentially endless pile of money in your lap? You probably haven't had to attack this problem before, but as they say in small-talk circles everywhere, "it's a good problem to have!"

We at StraightForward Interactive have attacked this problem dozens of times, and we've developed a pretty good system for maximizing the value of your Ad Grant. And what we mean when we say "maximizing the value" is simply to spend as much of the grant money as possible every day, and spend it on things that can make the biggest impact on your organization.

And thanks to a really cool anagramming website we found that figures out the catchiest words you can create out of the letters you have at your disposal, we've named it the "LIMBER UP" method. It's an appropriate name semantically speaking as well, because the tenets we explore here really do teach you how to be flexible with your Ad Grant and do things with it that you probably wouldn't have otherwise considered. (Thanks, Wordsmith.org!)

And not for nothing, "LIMBER" is less off-putting than "MR. BILE," which was the second coolest name we could make out of the same letters.

So let's get limber, shall we?

"L" IS FOR LIST BUILDING
As in, email lists.

If you ask 100 nonprofits with a Google Ad Grant what the ideal outcome of their participation in the program would be, at least 99% of them will say one thing: donations!

Of course they will. Why wouldn't they? Money makes the

world go 'round.

Unfortunately, donations are the toughest thing for any non-profit to snag, and that's true via Google Ad Grants as well. All too often, nonprofits are sold the idea – by Google itself in its promotional materials or by a smooth-talking agency salesperson – that you simply plug your organization into Google Ad Grants and all of the free advertising dollars it brings, and immediately, the monetary donations just start a-flowin'.

But that's not reality. The first thing to remember here is that people who find your nonprofit via a Google ad are very often seeing/hearing of your organization for the very first time. That's a critical point that you must remember: Until the moment they click on one of your ads, these people didn't know you existed. And what's the likelihood that someone who didn't know you existed a few seconds ago is likely to start handing you money moments later? Not very good.

Consider your in-person interactions with new people. How often do you meet new people, tell them you work for a non-profit and have them immediately open up their wallets and start handing you cold, hard cash? Never. And that's when they're right there looking you in the eye, without the luxury of being able to shut a laptop and make you go away. Instant donations don't happen in person, on the Web or anywhere else.

And that makes perfect sense. It's a crowded world out there, and there's no lack of people and organizations asking for money.

Thus, people need time and repeat exposure to become comfortable enough with your organization and mission to start loosening the purse strings, and that process takes time and action on your part. Google Ad Grants is awesome for introducing your nonprofit to the world, but the heavier lifting of teasing out donations, financial and otherwise, falls to you.

What can you do in order to facilitate this process? Build an email list!

If you took every item in our snazzy "LIMBER up" acronym and forced me to choose one of them as the *only* thing you were able to do with Google Ad Grants, email list-building is the one I'd choose. There are several reasons for this:

1. Signing up for your email list is a much smaller and more reasonable ask of the website visitor, far easier to acquire than a donation by orders of magnitude. It's a far more natural and realistic second step from a user who's had a brief look at your site and is at least mildly interested. If I'm mildly interested in what you've got going on at your nonprofit, I'm definitely warm to the idea of hearing more from you later on – far warmer than I am to whipping out my credit card just yet.

2. Once someone has signed up for your email list, you can communicate with them at will. Now, it goes without saying that the discipline of email marketing is an entire dinosaur unto itself, one you must use wisely. But for simplicity's sake,

we'll summarize it this way: Building an opt-in email list lets you communicate regularly with those who are most interested in your website and mission.

3. Using your Ad Grants account to build an email list is an ideal way to take first-time site visitors who may otherwise never return and turn them into a valuable marketing asset that you can revisit again and again for every marketing objective you have. You can tell them about new content on your website. Events you're hosting. Merchandise you're selling. Volunteer and internship opportunities. All of that stuff. And, when the time is right, asking for donations.

The single most important rule of list-building: Make it easy.

Don't kill the golden goose that list-building can be by asking for too much information in your opt-in form. I prefer two fields – name and email address – and that's it. No more. Resist, with every fiber of your being, the temptation to squeeze more and more data points out of your users, because the number of email signups decreases with every field you add to your form.

Call them lazy, frazzled, busy, spoiled or whatever you like, but the fact is that people just don't fill out long forms. One of our most well-heeled nonprofit clients has always ignored this advice and insisted on requiring nearly a dozen fields in their signup forms: not only name and email but job title, number of employees in the nonprofit, annual donation revenue, areas of societal interest, all that jazz. And guess what? Their opt-in rate (the rate at which people who visit the form actually complete the sign-up process) is pitiful.

As Grandma used to say, some people just have more money than sense. But if you're reading this book, that's not you. You're long on sense, so put all those brains to good use and don't ask for any more information in an email signup form than you absolutely require. The quicker and easier it is to fill out your opt-in form, the more quickly you'll build a robust list that you can tap repeatedly and to great effect.

"I" IS FOR INTERNS (AND VOLUNTEERS. AND EMPLOYEES. BUT LET'S START WITH INTERNS)

One of the most frequently overlooked ways to take advantage of Google Ad Grants is to use it as a recruiting tool. Sure, everyone wants monetary donations, but what about donations of time and manpower? Sometimes, the need for money is eclipsed by the need for people to chip in a few hours here and there, and Ad Grants can help with that as well.

Internships are a fascinating opportunity in the digital age. If you live near a college, you can rest assured that there are hundreds of students looking for an internship to bolster their résumés. But don't stop there.

Even if you don't live near a college, you're still in the game if you have work that can be done by "virtual" interns; that is to say, students from across the country, or even around the globe, who can do work for you and get that same résumé entry – without ever having to step foot in your office. If the nearby college has hundreds of internship-seeking students, those hundreds become millions when you broaden your focus to the whole country or even the entire globe.

Volunteers: In almost every geographic area where our agency has ever advertised, there is search volume for queries relating to local volunteering opportunities. ("Search volume" simply means that there's a decent number of people searching for a particular query. For example, "Kim Kardashian instagram photos" has VERY high search volume. By contrast, "Josh Barsch instagram photos" has no search volume whatsoever.)

You may not realize it, but there are a lot of people in your community who would love to keep themselves busy with some volunteer work but simply don't know which organizations need the help. Some don't even know where to start looking, and that's what has them on Google searching for things like "volunteer opportunities."

You can bid on these keywords, and you should! There isn't a warmer audience from which to recruit potential helpers than people who are searching for volunteer opportunities on Google at this very moment. They're aching to put their free time to use by helping organizations like yours!

Remember, the highest-performing ads will directly address the query that users have typed into Google. So if your user has just entered "volunteer opportunities in Memphis," your ad should say something like this:

> **Volunteer With Us In Memphis – We Need Lots Of Volunteers**
> **We're Recruiting Volunteers For Agencies All Over Memphis.**
> **Apply Today!**

Or how about:

> **Memphis Volunteers Wanted – You Can Apply Today**
> **Complete A Quick Form & Background Check & Start Volun-**
> **teering Now!**

Both of these are ads that you can reasonably presume will be attractive to people who are searching for volunteerism-related keywords.

Employees: You might be reading this book hot off the presses in late 2016, or maybe 2017, or 2019, or whatever. So at this very moment, the American economy could be going gangbusters, or it could be in shambles. But we can assure you that in either of those scenarios and in all scenarios in between, people will be looking for jobs, and they'll be looking for them on Google. Thus, if your nonprofit is hiring for positions of any kind, you can absolutely use your Ad Grant to advertise these job openings.

And trust us: Ads about job openings will drive significant traffic to your site. Some of the most effective campaigns we've ever run for our nonprofits here at StraightForward are help-wanted campaigns for positions ranging from entry-level clerical help all the way up to highly skilled health care positions requiring specialized graduate degrees. And the best part? The marketing cost to fill the positions is zero. Just a little bit of free advertising credit can do the job just fine. Thanks, Google!

"M" IS FOR MERCHANDISE

Selling merchandise is one of the greatest, most underused tactics that you can easily do with Google Ad Grants. A lot of nonprofits think you're not allowed to advertise products for sale with your Grants account, but you absolutely are. The only caveat is that 100% of your profits must go back to the charity, and I expect that's the case with most charities (who else would you be giving the profits to?).

But here's the thing: Even if you aren't giving 100% of your profits back to the charity, I have very deep doubts about Google's interest in checking, or even ability to check, whether you are doing so. Google Ad Grants is one of hundreds of initiatives/divisions within the company, and it's not one that attracts many internal resources. It doesn't make Google any money, and it never will. In fact, it's a total loss-leader. The only gain Google derives from the Ad Grants program is goodwill and good publicity. Hence, very little manpower is devoted to Google Ad Grants from within. Even basic account help is almost nonexistent.

If you want evidence of how asleep at the wheel Google is about its own Ad Grants program, cruise on over to the official website at www.google.com/grants and check out the "Grantspro" section. Grantspro was a wonderful program that would let highly successful current grantees upgrade to a much bigger monthly grant: $40,000 per month instead of just $10,000. But Grantspro was discontinued in September 2016, dashing the hopes of many a starry-eyed charity hoping for the big upgrade.

Nonetheless, there's a giant headline on the Ad Grants home page that bellows, "Step Up To Grantspro!" But directly underneath it, there's a paragraph that says, "The Ad Grants team is no longer accepting Grantspro applications." Ohhh-kay. Then why's there a big headline that says "Step Up To Grantspro"? Surely there's someone at Google who knows how to remove text from a web page, right?

Do you know what it would take to fix this immensely frustrating, mind-bogglingly amateurish user experience on the Ad Grants website? I'll tell you exactly: It would take three minutes, one human being with a beating heart and an eyedropper full of give-a-shit.

Google has plenty of people on the clock; it just pays so little attention to the Ad Grants program that even a comically absurd user experience like the one I've described above can sit unnoticed for months.

Now, back to the merchandise issue, here's the reason I point this out. If Google is so checked-out that it can't even be bothered to check its own website, do you think it's going to be actively policing whether you're giving 100% of your merchandise profits back to your charity? Highly, highly unlikely.

I'm not telling you to break the rules. You shouldn't; the potential upside of selling products you aren't allowed to sell doesn't outweigh the potential downside of losing your Ad Grant. I'm simply saying that I don't think this particular rule is policed very actively; thus, you should have no issues using your Ad Grants account to sell merchandise to your heart's content.

Another reason merchandise is an exciting usage of Ad Grant money is the fact that a lot of the merch that nonprofits sell happens to be stuff that's very low-margin and therefore doesn't attract a lot of for-profit competition on AdWords. Calendars, coffee cups, T-shirts, CDs, DVDs, etc.: These are low-margin items that are simply impossible for a lot of businesses to sell using AdWords. If a company sells a pack of pencils for $5, how many clicks can they possibly absorb on AdWords before they've spent more in advertising than the retail price of the pencils? Not very many, that's how many.

But wait. Let's say you're a nonprofit focused on LGBT rights, and you sell rainbow pencils emblazoned with your nonprofit's URL. You sell them for $10 a pack (hey, they're rainbow; you can price them at a bit of a premium). Let's say your production/wholesale costs are $3 a pack, so you have $7 of profit for each pack you sell.

Guess who can now afford to bid $2 per click? You can! Profitability? We don't need no stinkin' profitability! You can spend

$20 of Google's money on every pack of pencils you sell if you want – that's 500 packs of pencils sold, at $7 profit per pack – $3,500 in your nonprofit's bank account. Sweet!

Or let's say you're a pet-rescue nonprofit (we work with several of these), and you've produced a calendar full of adorable puppies that you sell (with 100% of the profits coming back to your organization, of course) for $10.

Other big for-profit publishers sell a similar calendar for $10 also. But they have margins to make. Can they afford to bid $2 a click on a calendar for which they make only $5 of profit on each sale? Absolutely not. Even if they sold a calendar on every third click, that's $6 of spend against $5 of margin. They're in the red. Not gonna work.

But can you? Absolutely! You can bid and absorb $2 clicks all day long, because you're not using real money. You're using Google's money, and you have $329 of it every day to spend how you like. Plus – bonus! – you have a much more compelling pitch to the searcher than your for-profit competitors do. Whom would you rather give your puppy-calendar money to: a huge publishing conglomerate or a real nonprofit that takes the money and uses it to care for the puppies in the calendar pictures? It's a no-brainer.

So let's do the math here for the puppy calendar project. Let's say you make a $10 puppy calendar that costs you $4 apiece in printing costs, for a $6-per-unit profit. Let's say you use your Ad Grant to bid on nothing but puppy-calendar-related stuff (because you can certainly do that if you want to).

Let's be more realistic and assume that your clicks cost you $1.75 apiece (having to pay the full $2 per click is rare). Let's also make the realistic, possibly conservative, assumption that out of all these people who are searching for "puppy calendar" and other such phrases indicating they want to buy exactly the type of puppy calendar you have, only 10% of them follow through and purchase one of your calendars after clicking an AdWords ad to check it out.

That's one calendar sold, and $6 of profit, for every $17.50 of your grant money spent. If you spend your entire $10,000 monthly grant this way, that's 571 calendars sold per month (for the mathematically challenged, that's $10,000 divided by $17.50). So 571 calendars at $6 of profit each equals $3,426 of profit. Per month!

Wow!

Those two examples probably explain very well why Google Ad Grants customers who sell merch excite me so much; it's a very nice way to monetize the grant, which keeps them very happy and more than willing to keep paying us our measly $400 monthly fee to manage their Ad Grants account!

If you don't currently sell any merchandise, the above scenario should make you rethink that and, if possible, add some merch to your offerings. Because what we've spelled out above is exactly this: By giving you an Ad Grant, Google is not only giving you advertising money, it's enabling you to create/manufacture merchandise profitably – merchandise that doesn't even exist yet.

Mindblowing stuff. Seems too good to be true, doesn't it? But it's true nonetheless. Long story short: Do not overlook merchandise when determining how to focus your Google Ad Grant marketing efforts.

ADVANCED TIP: Make sure that the "store" area of your nonprofit is located on your Ad Grants-approved domain and that it does NOT link off to another domain or store host. Remember that ads in your account *must* point to this domain, so you'll want to have your store URL be http://mynonprofitsmainurl.org/snugglypuppycalendarstore or http://mynonprofitsmainurl.org/rainbowpencilstore or something like that. If you link off to an eBay store or Amazon or any other hosted e-commerce platform, you're out of luck.

"B" IS FOR BRANDING

In the advertising world, you may hear "branding" defined a dozen ways, but we're sticking to the basics here. Much like a rancher presses his searing hot iron onto his horse's heavily muscled butt cheek, "branding" gets your organization's name out there in front of as many people as possible and leaves your distinct mark on the world.

Notice the two parts there: creating a distinct mark and spreading that mark as far and wide as you can. The distinct mark itself is up to you, and you've probably done this work already. What does your nonprofit do for the world? How does it do that? How is it different from others? Your elevator pitch answers those questions. But the Ad Grant is your tool for getting the word out to the masses.

And that's no easy task; the nonprofit world is a crowded one. The National Center for Charitable Statistics indicates that there are over 1.5 million registered nonprofits in the United States alone, and estimates suggest about five to 10 times that many throughout the world. And they're all competing with each other every day to bring attention, and of course dollars, to the causes for which they advocate.

Yowza.

If you have an Ad Grant, you've got a huge and immediate leg up on most of them, because most of them *don't* have an Ad Grant. Google itself claims that "over 100,000 nonprofits" participate; that's no more than 1 or 2 percent of all nonprofits worldwide that, like you, have $10,000 a month of free money, forever, to promote your cause.

So let's assume that you're a cancer charity. The various cancer charities of the world have many goals: They want to raise money for research, raise awareness, provide patient support or family support, provide palliative or hospice care, etc. And many more. But all of them, including our fictional example organization here, have one thing in common: cancer. (I know, I know. "Thank you, Captain Obvious." But give me some leash for a moment.)

The number of different search queries flowing into Google's servers each day containing the word "cancer" is in the millions. Trust me, I've seen them. Everything from "cancer treatments" to "ovarian cancer" to "does hemp oil cure cancer" to "chemotherapy nausea" to "aspartame causes cancer" to "patrick swayze pancreatic cancer" to "cancer zodiac ideal mate" ... the list is truly endless. When I say millions of unique queries, I do mean millions. And they're varied beyond imagination.

But, regardless of what your organization's specific angle on cancer is – research, awareness, family help – you're interested in reaching anyone who's searching for anything related to cancer. These people are all your people in some way, even if they're searching for a mission that's not specifically yours. Why? Because in nearly all cases, *they are people who are affected by cancer in some way.*

Now, if your organization provides support to single parents with cancer, you are obviously interested in reaching people searching for things like "parents with cancer" or "talking with children about cancer." But perhaps less obviously, you should also be interested in those searching for "newest cancer research" or "Mexico cancer centers." Why? Again, it's simple: These people are affected by cancer in some way. Maybe they themselves have cancer. Maybe it's a friend or a loved one.

Even if they aren't looking for your particular service, they may know someone who is. Cancer patients and families tend to develop relationships with other cancer patients and *their* families, and one of those families may in fact be looking for what you offer. Word spreads, and that's what you want.

So when we bring that into focus, the answer becomes much simpler when we ask ourselves, "As a cancer charity, do I want to reach all the people I can who are affected by cancer with a message about my organization and what we do?" Of course we do. That's the reason for our existence, right? The more people who know about our cancer charity, the more people we can serve.

And that's precisely the way you use Google Ad Grants to get your organization in front of thousands of new people every day: You go wide with your keyword selection. Very, very wide.

Our sample cancer charity shouldn't be bidding on mere dozens of keywords, or even hundreds, that are a very close match to the specific services we offer. No way. We're going wide; we should be bidding on tens of thousands of keywords, if not hundreds of thousands. We should be bidding on every last cancer-related search that our keyword tools can generate for us, and then some. (Well, except searches related to the Cancer zodiac sign. Those, we can stand to pass over.)

It makes sense, right? Anybody who's Google searching anything about cancer is someone we'd like to know about our cancer charity. Plain and simple.

But that's not the only reason we go wide.

We also go wide because there are a lot of cancer charities out there with Google Ad Grants accounts. Furthermore, the biggest players not only have Ad Grants accounts, they also have separate paid AdWords accounts, where they're allowed to bid as high as they like on any keyword they like, a virtual arsenal of advertising ammo that blows regular nonprofits out of the water.

What's that mean? It means that when we're bidding on the most popular cancer-related keyword phrases, our ads are probably never going to show up. The big boys will outspend us by a huge margin, squeezing us out of those top positions.

How do we get around that and still get $329 worth of our message out to the world every day? By going wide. It's a numbers game, really. If we're bidding on only 250 popular cancer-related keywords, the likelihood is very high that other organizations will be bidding on them as well, and many of them will outrank us. So our ads won't show up, and we won't get any traffic to our website.

In short, we've got that new Cadillac with no engine.

But if we bid on 250,000 cancer-related phrases, the likelihood of us being outgunned is very low. The more keywords we bid on, the better our chances for exposure and subsequent success. Or, to use the language of my favorite motivational quote: "To be successful, you have to be willing to do what the other guy won't."

From deep experience, I can tell you that very, very few of the other guys – other nonprofits, in this case – are going wide. Your competitors in this advertising space skew heavily toward the 250-keyword accounts, not the 250,000-keyword accounts. This is your opportunity; this is where you can win. Going wide – wider than the other guy is willing to go – is the key to maximizing your Ad Grant and spending $329 every day.

But wait, there's more.

Thus far, when we've talked about "exposure," we've been talking about the people the Ad Grant brings to your website. That's the goal, of course, and that's how you spend your $329 each day; people click on your ads, each click costs you "money," and when your daily allotment of $329 has been used up by ad clicks, your account goes to sleep and wakes up at midnight with a fresh $329 to spend.

But let's not forget about "impressions." An impression is simply the single, one-time display of your ad on a Google search-results page. When your ad is shown to somebody, somewhere, that's an impression.

Google doesn't charge you for ad impressions; it charges you only when someone clicks on your ad. So if your ad accrues 100 impressions and only two people click on it, you pay for only those two. The other 98 people who saw your ad? You got those for free.

And you'll always get them for free; in search advertising,

impressions are always free. And a well-managed, fully spending Ad Grants accounts will accrue well over 1 million ad impressions in a year, often more.

Is an impression as valuable as a click? Of course not. The person who clicks through and checks out your website is far more valuable to you. But do impressions, without clicks, have any value whatsoever? Does having a million people see your ad deliver more value than having zero people see your ad?

OK, I loaded the question there a bit. Of course impressions have value. Of course having your message in front of millions is better than having it in front of nobody, even if a majority of those millions don't click their way through to your website.

It's the identical concept used by our aging brethren in TV, print and outdoor media: exposures, exposures, exposures. Repeat exposures drill your message into people's consciousness, even if they're not engaging with you right now and even if they never do. Those incessant political TV ads, those cheesy real estate billboards you drive by every day – they may not be pretty, and most of the time they may not interest you, but they get the job done. They burn the message into your head through massive exposure.

We point this out because using your Ad Grant to build exposure for your nonprofit is one of the easiest benefits to take advantage of but also the most overlooked. A vast majority of nonprofits judge the success of their Ad Grants campaigns solely by the highest-value conversion actions (donations, sales, volunteering commitments, etc.). And although those are, by all means, the most important and easily trackable outcomes, don't forget the incredible power of spreading the word!

"E" IS FOR EVENT PROMOTION

Merchandise may be the most overlooked opportunity in the Ad Grants world, but event promotion has to be a close second. Let me tell you a story.

One of our cancer-charity clients was plugging along without much new content or direction in their AdWords account for a couple of months. Cancer charities are notoriously tough to manage, because there are so, so many of them, and they all bid on the same keywords, and when 2,000 cancer charities are bidding on the same cancer-related keywords for a mere four ad positions, most of them come up empty. So I click over to the website just to check out what's going on with the organization, and lo and behold, what do I find? A very famous rock musician – one of my personal favorites, actually – was doing a benefit concert for my client. IN THREE DAYS.

Man! Talk about a missed opportunity! We could've been using the Google Ad Grants account to advertise that show for MONTHS to generate awareness of the show, to sell tickets, to get good publicity for both the artist and the charity, etc. But we never got the chance, because the client never told us about the show. When I mentioned it to the executive director, she just said, "Gosh, I'm sorry. I didn't know we were allowed to advertise that."

Yes, you certainly are! If you're holding events that benefit your organization, you're absolutely allowed to use the Ad Grants account to advertise them.

And every Ad Grants advertising manager loves special events. LOVES them. They introduce an entirely new set of eligible keywords that we can now bid on in order to drive traffic to the website. And not just any traffic – NEW traffic, new people who have probably never heard of the charity and certainly haven't been to the website.

Let's say the band I mentioned above for the cancer charity event was Metallica (it wasn't Metallica). If Metallica is now playing a charity concert in Los Angeles for my cancer organization, and my cancer organization has a page on its website devoted to the event, I can now bid on thousands of new and relevant terms in my Ad Grants account, such as:

- Metallica
- Rock concerts
- Live music
- Los Angeles music
- Things to do in Los Angeles

… and hundreds of similar variants. Now, would I ever bid on "Metallica" if I were a for-profit advertiser? Absolutely not, not even if I was selling Metallica concert tickets (The word "Metallica" doesn't signal any particular intent on the searcher's part, so even if I were selling concert tickets, there's no way this keyword would be profitable for me).

But I can do it with an Ad Grants account, because it's Google's money I'm spending, not mine.

Now, the skeptic might say, "Well, that's kind of an under-handed way to get traffic to the charity's website; none of those keywords have anything to do with curing cancer."

And to that I'd say, you're out of your mind.

Metallica doesn't have anything to do with cancer, either, but like EVERY SINGLE OTHER FUNDRAISER IN THE HISTORY OF FUNDRAISERS, the event is designed to use one popular thing (in this case, Metallica) in order to attract attention and awareness to another less-popular thing that needs more support (in this case, cancer research). Would you criticize a nonprofit for hanging flyers, placing a magazine ad or running a radio spot to a mass audience of mostly-uninterested people in the hopes of catching the interest of a few? Of course you wouldn't. So it's absurd to make the criticism of using Ad Grants in the same fashion.

Another example: One of our clients, a crisis-counseling organization, was hosting a very large and very fancy chocolate festival as a fundraiser one spring. Dozens of local chefs, restaurateurs and confectioners were signed up and were all bringing truckloads of gourmet chocolate desserts, and if you bought a $20 ticket, you were free to partake all evening long.

It was pretty incredible. Writing about it still makes me hungry to this day.

Back at the agency, we pounced on the opportunity the moment we learned of it. We bid on every chocolate-related keyword we could find. Every dessert-related keyword we could find. If it was a noun and it contained refined sugar, we probably bid on it.

Our rationale was simple: If someone in the area is searching for a "chocolate cake recipe," they are very likely to be interested in my nonprofit's chocolate festival. It's not exactly a stretch to think so. Now, replace "chocolate cake recipe" with any of 10,000 other sweets-related phrases, and you've got an Ad Grants account running at full capacity, sending thousands of people to the website and eventually hundreds to what turned out to be a very successful event for our client.

It's probably becoming clear, then, that events are a great usage of your Ad Grant money. But what you may not realize is how this practice can help inform what events you plan in the future for maximum impact to your organization. If you know what keywords people in your area frequently search for, you can realize some great piggybacking opportunities off those keywords by holding events associated with them.

I (Josh) live in Rapid City, S.D. One of the main venues for outdoor fun in the spring, summer and even into the fall is something called Main Street Square. It's one square block in the middle of town that has boutique shopping, restaurants, an ice-skating rink when it's cold and fountains when it's warm, an amphitheatre for families to come watch movies and plays, etc. Everyone who lives in my town knows where Main Street Square is, and especially during the warm months, you can be certain that a lot of local people will be Googling "Main Street Square" to find out what events are happening there.

In addition to that, we have a block party near Main Street Square every Thursday night in the summertime called Summer Nights (the name may not be creative, but it's still a good time). There's a concert by a different band every week, which leads to a lot of people searching for "Summer Nights" throughout the entire season.

Now, let's say you're a nonprofit organization in my town, and you have the option of holding some type of fundraising event at Main Street Square or another, lesser-known (and most important, less-often-searched) venue. I'm sure there are pros and cons to each, but if you have a Google Ad Grant, a significant pro for Main Street Square would be the volume of people searching for "Main Street Square" all summer, people whose searches I can piggyback onto and get major exposure for my event that otherwise I wouldn't get. I can write a Google ad that says:

Main Street Square
Bring The Kids & Face-Paint With
Us July 4th At Main Street Square!

This is great for me, for several reasons:

1. Everyone who searches for "Main Street Square" – for whatever reason – is going to see my ad, getting me a ton of free exposure for my event. Remember, the clicks may be free, but exposure is doubly free. I don't even use any of my free Google ad credit when someone looks at my ad; I spend it only when they click.
2. A lot of these people – not a majority by any means, but some – will click through to my site and learn more about the event and my organization.
3. This ad will rank better than most for the keyword "Main Street Square," because I was able to squeeze the keyword into both the headline and the body of the ad. Google likes and rewards that.

And notice how, in my ad text, I'm not groveling for a donation or even mentioning the name of my charity at all. I'm just telling people about a fun upcoming event at a place they're already searching for. If I'd elected to have my event in the basement of an old church or something, I wouldn't be able to capture all these eyeballs.

Now, back to the Summer Nights example. We can apply the same principle here, but our "intervention" into the search results is even sneakier, because Summer Nights is a pretty tightly controlled block party, and it's unlikely that you'd even be able, let alone allowed, to hold a charity event right in the middle of it. But if one of my clients is holding an event anywhere near

Summer Nights, guess what keyword I'm bidding on? That's right: Summer Nights.

That's where my event is (close enough for me, anyway), and the Summer Nights merry-makers are the exact crowd I'd like to reach. If I'm having my fundraiser on the next block over from the Summer Nights shindig, I'll happily write an ad that says:

Headed To Summer Nights?
Bring Two Cans Of Food & Support
Helping Hands Homeless Shelter.

Again, will every Summer Nights searcher bring some food? Nope. But plenty of them will click my ad to see what it's all about. And they'll see what it's about immediately, by the way, because I'll make sure the ad takes them straight to a page talking about my food-donation fundraiser. Not my home page, not my donate page, a page that talks specifically about the event I'm trying to bring people to.

Will the ability to capture low-hanging Google search traffic always make the difference in the events you choose to hold and the locations you use to hold them? Probably not every time, but it's always something to keep in mind, because it can make a huge difference in the turnout and success of your events.

"R" IS FOR RETARGETING

Retargeting? What's that? Let's back up here a moment so the uninitiated among you can get your bearings.

FORESHADOWING ALERT: This section contains a catch, and then another catch. Prepare yourself!

Retargeting – also known as "remarketing" – is, in layman's terms, the act of following people around the Internet with your ads after they've visited your site. You're probably quite familiar with retargeting even if you don't necessarily know it by name.

Has this ever happened to you? You're hanging out on Amazon for a while one day, just browsin', maybe checking out one of those fancy Ninja blenders (Have you seen those things? They're awesome. I think mine could shred an empty beer can into in a fine powder.). For whatever reason, you are insufficiently impressed by the Ninja (your loss, pal), and you leave Amazon.com without buying one. But a few days later, when you're back at your computer browsing other websites, you start noticing Amazon ads for that same exact blender popping up all over the Internet, wherever you go.

The Ninja is following you. It's now a sentient kitchen robot that won't stop its pursuit of you until you agree to let it into your home.

OK, not really. But it's not an accident. It's retargeting.

Retargeting is the toast of the online advertising industry these days, and understandably so. Many studies have shown that most people don't buy (or donate, or fill out forms, or whatever it is you want them to do) on the first exposure to your website or ad. The more exposures they have to your ad, the more likely they are to act. So who wouldn't like a second, or third, or eighth or ninth crack at that potential customer once they've left the site and decided not to buy something, or do something that you wanted them to do?

Remarketing lets you "hold on" to that website visitor and continue showing them ads longer than you could've done before, days, weeks or even months after they've visited your website.

It's a marketer's dream. And like many marketers' dreams, it was a little bit creepy for consumers at the outset – a little Big Brother-ish for some people's tastes. But retargeting has been around for many years, and people are accustomed to it. File it under the same category as when I walk into Walgreens and my phone vibrates in my pocket to show me the current weekly ad. Like most advertising innovations of the digital age, it's creepy at first, but if it's ultimately helpful, people accept it.

Another element of remarketing that makes it so attractive is the price tag: It's extremely cheap. You might be wondering how that's possible; one would naturally think that such an extremely targeted audience – people who have showed interest in your organization by visiting your website – would command a serious premium. But the opposite is true. Understanding why takes a little explanation, but stay with me. It's not too complicated, and it's totally worth understanding!

When you visit a website, that website drops a "cookie" on your computer. Cookies are old news on the Internet; they keep track of your browsing history. So you're visiting Amazon.com, let's say, and Amazon "drops" a cookie on your website. (I think they called it that because, well, everyone loves cookies. If they called it a "Brussels sprout," people might've resisted it more.) The cookie knows exactly what pages of Amazon's website you've visited.

At the same time, Amazon is buying ad space on other websites. Lots of them. For the purposes of this explanation, we're going to use CNN.com. So when you're visiting CNN.com, the CNN website will look for an Amazon cookie on your computer before it decides what ads it will show alongside the news story you're about to read. And if the CNN site checks your computer and does indeed find an Amazon cookie, CNN.com will show you an ad for that fine Ninja blender you were checking out at Amazon just a short time ago.

That's a massively oversimplified explanation of retargeting, but I'm keeping it simple so that you understand the next part. Remember a few sentences ago when I said that remarketing ads target *only* people who are previous visitors to your site? Well, as you can imagine, the people who have visited your organization's website are a very, very, VERY small fraction of the vast expanse of the internet-using public that can be targeted with ads.

So let's think about CNN again for a second. Prior to the advent of retargeting, you could, in theory, try to follow your previous website visitors around with ads, namely the ones who went on to visit CNN.com. But to do so, you'd have to pay the market rate for advertising on CNN's website, competing with all other advertisers worldwide who also want to advertise on CNN, which makes their ad rates astronomical. And of course, you'd have to cross your fingers and say a little prayer that a lot of your previous website visitors actually happened to be visiting CNN.com after visiting your site.

This, of course, is absurd and would sink you into bankruptcy immediately. You'd have to outbid all other advertisers across the globe for that ad space on CNN.com – and oh, by the way, only a few dozen of your site visitors actually made it over to CNN.com anyhow, so 99.99999% of the people you spent that kajillion dollars advertising to, they didn't know who the heck you were and thus didn't click on your ads. But you're bankrupt nonetheless, because guess what? If you were buying ads directly from CNN, it's not like Google, where impressions are free and you pay only when people click on your ads. Nope. You pay per impression. No free impressions here. And of course, when those tens of millions of worldwide visitors flow into CNN.com, 99.9999% of whom don't know who your nonprofit is and have no interest in clicking on your ads, you still rack up the advertising charges.

Booooo.

Lather, rinse and repeat the above paragraph for every other high-dollar website that your site visitors may frequent: The New York Times, Yahoo, LinkedIn, Reddit, etc.

Not feasible, to say the least.

But now, enter retargeting. Retargeting allows you to say, "Yes, I absolutely want to advertise on CNN.com, NYTimes.com, Yahoo.com, LinkedIn.com and Reddit.com. All of 'em. But I only want my ad to appear on those websites when they're being looked at by someone who's recently visited my organization's website."

Now, that's a whole different kettle of fish. A horse of a different color. Or whatever phrase your grandpa taught you about something that's entirely different from the previous thing being discussed.

So, here's our situation now: While the Times and CNN and Yahoo and all those other websites put together have tens or hundreds of millions of monthly visitors, we automatically get to eliminate the 99.9999% of them who are unfamiliar with your organization.

Poof. They're gone. Retargeting waves a giant, ultrapowerful magnet over the top of the Texas-size haystack of internet traffic, sucks up all of your previous site visitors, throws them into a retargeting "list" and lets you advertise only to them, wherever they go – even those big, popular websites.

And that makes it extremely cheap to advertise to them. Why?

Simple: Because, relatively speaking, there's not very many of them. Heck, advertising gets expensive only when you're showing it to a lot of people. Let's say you've got a retargeting list of 5,000 previous site visitors that you'd like to continue advertising to on other sites. In advertising terms, 5,000 visitors is peanuts. Using retargeting campaigns, you can get in front of 5,000 people for around $5 a day.

OK, I know you're impatiently waiting to find out what the catches are, and I'm about to tell you the first one. Promise me you won't be mad. (I trust that you nodded, however cautiously.)

CATCH 1: YOU CAN'T USE RETARGETING IN AN AD GRANTS ACCOUNT

I know, I know! You're thinking, "Then why on earth did you spend the last few pages explaining how to use retargeting if we can't use it in our Ad Grants account?" And it's true: Ad Grants accounts can be used only for search advertising, which again means you can target people only by the phrases they search for on Google, not whether they've been to your website before or any other way.

But never say die, because …

CATCH 2: YOU CAN STILL USE RETARGETING – OUT OF A SEPARATE, PAID ADWORDS ACCOUNT

Google strictly prohibits its advertisers from using multiple

AdWords accounts to advertise their products and services, but one group of advertisers enjoys an exemption from that rule: nonprofits with Ad Grants accounts. Nonprofits are allowed (and encouraged!) to open a second, paid account. This makes sense: Google loves revenue, and just because it's given you a free Ad Grants account doesn't mean it wouldn't love for you to spend some of your extra cash there, too.

And you should – even if it's just for retargeting. Retargeting is an extremely cheap way to get *back* in front of all those free visitors that your Ad Grants account has given you, over and over and over again.

Of all the tips in this book, this is probably the most secret-weapon-ish that we have to offer (which is why I spent all that hot air explaining retargeting before; it's worth going the extra mile to get the big benefits of doing what the other guy won't). Almost no one does this, and I've never heard or seen the advice given elsewhere. It truly is your clickbait-style "TRANSFORM YOUR NONPROFIT'S ADVERTISING WITH THIS ONE SECRET TRICK!" tactic.

Only a handful of nonprofits that we at StraightForward have ever worked with have operated a second account at all, usually due to budget constraints or the fact that they can't find a way to spend the $10,000 a month they've been given, let alone more. Those that have employed paid accounts have usually been very well-funded organizations whose operations much resemble those of for-profit businesses, and they've used those accounts for even more high-dollar search advertising.

But opening a paid account for remarketing is affordable for all nonprofits, regardless of size or budget. This isn't an exaggeration: If you can spend one dollar per day on a remarketing campaign, it's money well spent. For one stinking dollar, you can get your ads back in front of about 1,000 previous visitors and re-engage them with your organization.

Let's do an easy step-by-step here of how you can use a paid retargeting account hand in hand with an Ad Grants account:

1. Open a paid AdWords account. (Just open it. You don't have to spend any money yet.)
2. From the paid account, copy the Google-provided "remarketing code" and place it on every page of your website.
3. Switch gears for a sec and hop over to your Ad Grants account. Get it firing on all cylinders, spending the full $329 each day, either via learning and implementing all the priceless strategies and tactics you'll learn in this book or by hiring an agency that knows all this stuff.
4. Due to your flawless execution of item 3 above, you're now sending hundreds of new visitors to your site each day. While that happens – because you dutifully placed your remarketing code, per item 2 – your paid account is automatically tracking and stockpiling each of those new visitors in a remarketing list for you to use for advertising purposes at a later date. By the time you pay your next electric bill, this list should contain thousands of people.

5. Start a retargeting campaign from your paid account targeting your fresh new list of recent site visitors and pull them back into your website for additional engagement. Set your campaign to spend no more than $5 a day if you want a small, low-risk test.

It really is that easy!

There you have it: Retargeting lets you leverage all the free traffic you get from your Ad Grants account in order to bring the most interested people back to your website over and over again – for pennies on the dollar.

And now, my friends, you are fully limbered up. To recap:

"L" is for list-building. Keep these zero-cost Ad Grants visitors in your marketing funnel by making it easy to sign up for your email list with a simple form.

"I" is for interns (and volunteers and employees). If your organization can benefit from extra manpower in any form, target keywords that indicate people are searching for jobs, internships or volunteer opportunities.

"M" is for merchandise. Use your Ad Grant to sell merchandise. If you don't have merchandise to sell, consider creating some!

"B" is for branding. Go wide with your keyword selection to get your organization and message in front of as many people as possible.

"E" is for event promotion. Use your Ad Grant to publicize every event you put on!

"R" is for retargeting. Retargeting requires a separate, paid AdWords account, but the costs are extremely low, and the benefits are worth it!

Now you know how to use your Ad Grant to great effect. Next, let's explore how to lose it. Or, more accurately, how to *not* lose it.

THE TEN (OR SO) GOOGLE AD GRANTS COMMANDMENTS

(Or, "Rules You Must Follow So That Google Does Not Smite Thee")

The Google Ad Grants program is certainly an example of a large corporation doing well by doing good. Google gives away tens of billions of advertising impressions every day for the benefit of more great causes than you could ever count.

Is that a benevolent overlord or what?

But make no mistake: A benevolent overlord is still an overlord. And like all legitimate overlords, Google will smite you in a heartbeat if you run afoul of its rules. If you screw up – accidentally or on purpose – Google doesn't want to hear any excuses. You don't get an appeal. There's no supervisor you can talk to. You're just out of luck.

And in the blink of an eye, your organization no longer has a perpetual $10,000-a-month advertising grant. And it's not better to have loved and lost than never to have loved at all. Having

$329 in free money to spend each day and then having it taken away because you didn't follow the rules – I'm pretty sure that feels worse than never getting the Grant to begin with.

In light of all that, I really can't emphasize this enough: Don't break the rules. First, though, you have to know what they are.

Rules for being accepted into the Google Ad Grants program:

Thou shalt hold valid charity status. In the US, that means you have to be an IRS-registered 501(c)(3). Outside the US, Google provides guidelines for every eligible country on the Ad Grants website (www.google.com/grants). And as of late 2016, Google is now requiring all nonprofits in every participating country – even the US – to validate their organizations with TechSoup.org, so if you haven't done that and you're planning on getting an Ad Grant, get cracking over at TechSoup so that you can be ready when it's time to apply.

Thou shalt acknowledge and agree to Google's required certifications regarding nondiscrimination and donation receipt and use. This means several things. First, you can't illegally discriminate against anyone in your hiring practices. Second, you can't discriminate against anyone based on sexual orientation or gender identity (even if there's no law against doing so in your area). Third – well, I'll just quote Google on this one:

"[Your] organization may receive this donation under

its own policy and applicable laws and regulations; this donation will not negatively impact Google's current or future ability to do business with [your] organization; and this donation will not be used to corruptly influence any government official to obtain or retain business or any improper advantage."

Huh. I've never heard of an Ad Grant being used to corrupt a government official, but Google apparently knows something we don't. OK, then, take note: No using your Ad Grant for coups, revolutions, juntas, overthrowing a dictator (benevolent or evil, doesn't matter, apparently), bribes, kickbacks or any other governmental corruption!

Thou shalt have a live website with substantial content. Don't let this one send you into a panic. By "substantial content," Google doesn't mean you need an archive of 300 useful news articles; in fact, in our experience, the bar for "substantial content" is painfully low. If you've got a bare-bones, five- or six-page website with your standard navigation items (Home, About Us, What We Do, Contact Us, yada yada yada) and fully built pages behind each of those links, you should pass the "substantial content" test with flying colors.

Thy website must be on its own domain. We run into this problem only occasionally, but it's worth mentioning. On the off chance that you've built your nonprofit's entire web presence on some sort of community web hub or a subdomain of a large-scale webhost, you won't be approved for Google Ad Grants. For example, if you're the executive director of Acme Widgets Inc. and your website is acmewidgets.org, you're in fine shape. But if your website is acmewidgets.wordpress.com or sites.google.com/site/acmewidgets, you're in bad shape. Not gonna happen.

However, if this is your situation, it's pretty easy to fix. A domain name costs about $10, and for about $50 to $100, you can have a professional re-create your existing site on your newly purchased domain. Super easy. You should do this anyway; you do not want your nonprofit's entire web presence to be built on what's essentially the "rented land" of a provider like this. You never know when they'll fold up and go out of business or get sold to another company. Much better to build your own website and have complete control!

Thou shalt not be a governmental entity/organization, hospital or medical group, school, child care center, academic institution or university. However, philanthropic arms of educational institutions (which generally are separate organizations with their own tax ID numbers) are, in fact, eligible. It's pretty self-explanatory: If you are any of these things, you're not going to get a Google Ad Grant. Google doesn't make its own independent determination of what type of organization you are; it simply takes your organization's tax ID number and checks to see what NTEE (National Taxonomy of Exempt Entities) code is associated with your organization. If your NTEE code tags you as one of the non grata organization types, you won't be approved.

Thou shalt link your ads to one (and only one) website domain, which should be the same one that was approved in your initial application. I'd call this one analogous to "Thou Shalt Not Covet," in that this is the commandment that everyone breaks. But you're forgiven, due to the fact that Almighty Google is a bit misleading here, because you're actually *allowed* to use multiple domains, as long as you ask first. Yes, you read that correctly: Google declares that you may use one and only one domain and then, immediately afterward, offers you the ability to use multiple other domains as long as you ask nicely. You simply go here to do so:

https://support.google.com/grants/contact/grants_v

Due in no small part to the fact that Google growls and puffs up its chest about using only one domain, nothing makes our non-profit clients happier than when we tell them that yes, Virginia, you can actually use other websites that you own and operate. And the better news is this: Google almost never, ever says no to requests sent through this form. I'm spitballing here, but I'd say out of 80 or 90 requests we've made for an additional domain to be approved, we've been denied once. In that instance, the domain our client was requesting was overtly commercial: It was a merchandise store without any mention of where the profits went. But every other request for an additional domain has been approved.

Having said that, it's important to note that we've submitted only sites that were clearly owned by our nonprofit clients and were clearly created around a separate initiative or event within our client's purview. The biggest and most common example of this would be 5Ks, fun runs, bike races, that kind of thing. Nonprofits frequently create entirely separate websites for those, because that makes entirely good sense. We've never been denied a request to add one of these sites to our Ad Grants account.

Thou shalt actively manage your AdWords account by logging in once a month and making at least one change to your account every 90 days. Pretty self-explanatory, but it's a critical point and worth a few sentences. Logging in and making a change once every three months is certainly no difficult task; even the busiest of folks can create five minutes here and there once a quarter. However, 90 days is enough time that the Ad Grants account can drift out of your mind. Having to do something once every three months isn't frequent enough to keep it in your mind at all, in my opinion – and that's what makes this very liberal rule a little dangerous. My advice? Set a calendar reminder on the first of each month to take five minutes to log into your account and make a change, even if it's just changing a keyword bid from $2.00 to $1.99. If you let that 90 days pass without making a change, every subsequent minute is a chance for Google to swoop in and disable your account permanently, kicking you out of the program altogether.

Thy (Thy? Thine? I'm terrible at Bible talk.) *ads and keywords should match your organization's programs and services.* This too is a very liberal guideline that, frankly, isn't strictly policed, if it's policed at all. Google is very tight-lipped about which and how many of its employees are keeping a strict eye on what you're doing with your Ad Grants account, so nobody knows for sure. But after years of managing many Ad Grants accounts and bidding on many millions of keywords, my educated guess is this: Google enforces the "relevant" keywords goal only reactively, not proactively. I think that, in theory, you could be bidding on any keyword under the sun, from "Donald Trump's toupee" to "Kim Kardashian's hair," and never be punished – unless a third party makes Google aware via a complaint.

But I absolutely don't recommend that. Google Ad Grants is a wonderful thing – a golden goose, as it were. There's absolutely no sense in getting greedy about keywords and putting your Grant at risk for, at best, a temporary benefit. Stick to keywords that are related to what your nonprofit is doing, and you should have no problems.

At the same time, don't be needlessly skittish. Let's say my nonprofit client is the Palookaville Boys and Girls Club. Let's then say that the PBGC is putting on a huge fundraiser shindig called "A Taste of Palookaville." All of Palookaville's finest restaurants will be providing their most sophisticated haute cuisine. The top Palookaville sommeliers will be there offering Palookaville's finest wines. Heck, even the Palookaville Culinary Institute and its top chefs will be there serving up stunning dishes.

Now, it's true that fine dining, food and wine are not part of the institutional mission of the Palookaville Boys and Girls Club. So is it appropriate for me to bid on keywords ranging from "Palookaville restaurants" to "fine dining Palookaville" to "wine stores in Palookaville," etc.?

Absolutely. These keywords are directly related to the PBGC's event, and those people represent the warmest and largest potential audience for my event, so that's what I'm going to bid on! The people looking to buy fine wine are right in my wheelhouse for a food and wine event. So are the people searching for fine dining. Of course I'm going to bid on them, and Google hasn't given me one iota of trouble for doing so over the course of nearly 10 years managing Ad Grants accounts.

Now, will I bid on those keywords year-round? After the event is over? Nope. That'd be pushing the envelope. But if I've got an event coming up involving food and wine, I'm going to bid far and wide on keywords related to food and wine.

Thou shalt not use strictly commercial advertising. If you're promoting products or services, 100% of the proceeds must go directly to supporting your program. That's the letter of Google's law on merchandise and other commercial advertising from within an Ad Grants account. But there's more there than meets the eye.

With such a stern declaration – "100% of the profits must go directly to supporting your program!" – one would think that Google's going to ask you for some serious documentation to prove this is the case before it lets you turn on advertising that's pointing to products for sale. But the fact is, it doesn't. Google may be one of the most prodigious collectors of behavioral information on the planet, but I'm sorry – it has no clue under the sun whether 100%, or even 1%, of the profits your organization makes from selling merchandise goes to supporting your program or to stocking your secret company bar with high-end liquor or to funding FARC rebels in Colombia. It just doesn't know, and I've never seen any mechanism by which it even attempts to check. By all appearances, you're on the honor system.

Please do not take this as my invitation to unscrupulously break the program rules by using your merchandise for anything other than your program. You shouldn't do that. I'm simply saying: If you think you're going to have to prove to some random Google employee that all your T-shirt money is going back into the general fund, that isn't going to happen.

Thou shalt not link your ads to pages that are primarily composed of links to other websites. This rule is in place so that you don't make an end-run around the rule about sending Ad Grants traffic only to your own website. Let's say your organization has partnered with Uber, and Uber's going to give two free rides to anyone who donates $25 to your organization. But the page where people can redeem this offer is on the Uber website, not yours. You're not allowed to send traffic directly to the Uber website, but hey! What if you create a page on your own website that's nothing but one big link to Uber? Can't do that either, and that's what this rule is designed to prevent.

Thou shalt not offer financial products like mortgages or credit cards in your ads, nor canst thou request donations of cars, boats or other property. We don't know why this particular rule is in place, honestly, but you can be sure that someone once found a way to exploit the Ad Grants program to turn big cash profits. It's true what they say; one bad apple spoils the whole damned bunch, and now you can't advertise any of these things. Sorry.

Thine website shalt not display Google AdSense ads or affiliate adver-tising links. This one is pretty straightforward. Google doesn't want to give you $10,000 worth of free advertising each month so that you can send the traffic right back out the door to exter-nal websites for a profit. Note the specific mention of Google AdSense and affiliate advertising programs. Other advertising, such as fixed-position sponsorships that you've sold independently, are permitted.

That's quite a few rules. So, what happens if you break one or two? Whatcha gonna do about it, Google?

Ad Grantees found in violation of any of these guidelines are subject to removal from the program. Google reserves the right to grant or deny an organization's application or participation at any time, for any reason, and to supplement or amend these eligibility guidelines at any time. Selections are made at Google's sole discretion and are not subject to external review.

Please read and reread the above paragraph and understand that this is not meaningless boilerplate. When Google says "Selections are made at Google's sole discretion and are not subject to external review," it absolutely means it. I know that we've alluded to certain policies that are lightly policed at best, but make no mistake: You should follow the rules. If you remember only one thing from this book, remember this: Google has no scruples whatsoever about pulling the plug on rulebreakers at any time, with zero notice. It is the lord and master of the program. It owes you nothing and answers to no one. There is no appeals process. There's no number to call and talk your way out of trouble. And it absolutely DOES. NOT. CARE. how much good your nonprofit does for the world when it comes to begging your way out of trouble. If you break the rules, Google will put your lights out faster than Travis shot Old Yeller, but without the tears.

Old Yeller was sad. We don't need any more sad in the world.

So keep your nose clean and follow the rules, and enjoy a bounty of free advertising money for years to come!

STRATEGIES FOR DOMINANCE

(Or, "How to Lubricate Your Engine")

OK, my friends, the baby-stuff section is now over. You're no longer an Ad Grants toddler; you're a grown adult who's ready for the big-time, advanced, not-found-anywhere-else strategies coming next.

This is the good stuff, so roll up your sleeves and get your highlighter ready. Unless you're reading this on a Kindle or a mobile device. Don't smear highlighter on those.

USE ADDITIONAL URLS IF YOU HAVE THEM

Google explicitly instructs Ad Grantees that they may send ad traffic only to the URL they provided in their initial Ad Grants application. This is a giant bummer for the many nonprofits that operate multiple websites dedicated to different areas of their mission. Some of StraightForward's nonprofit clients have a handful of separate websites; others have more than 50. But hey, tough luck, right? You have to pick just one.

As I mentioned before, you actually don't. There's a little-known application deep within the Ad Grants help system that allows you to submit a request for a second URL to be used with your ads. And a third. And a fourth. And so on. It's called the Ad Grants Additional Website(s) Domain form, and any Ad Grantee can use it. You simply submit your additional URL for approval along with an explanation of why you're making the request, and that's that. Google will usually respond within 24 hours, and it almost always says yes.

You can find it here:
https://support.google.com/grants/contact/grants_v

OVERLOAD YOUR KEYWORDS

For professional AdWords managers, Google Ad Grants is a strange beast. Though building a successful Ad Grants account requires expertise with and use of many of the same standard practices and techniques that are used with for-profit accounts, the manner in which you should employ those techniques is often entirely opposite of the way you'd manage a for-profit account.

There's no better example of this concept than keyword selection. With both for-profit AdWords and nonprofit Ad Grants, selecting good keywords is critical. With for-profit accounts, a good manager explores new keyword veins (around StraightForward, we call them "semantic buckets") and rigorously tests them to determine whether behind these keywords lurk people who are truly interested in their product or service. But the level and aggressiveness of these tests has to be tempered by the fact that every ad click sucks money out of our pockets and into Google's, regardless of whether they turn into customers on our end.

But with Google Ad Grants, that's not true at all. You can test whatever you please with no repercussions whatsoever, because you're not spending real money; you're spending Google's "house money." Put another way: If you're taking a date to an expensive restaurant but you're low on cash and footing the bill, you might order just enough food to fill your belly without making yourself look cheap. But if Bill Gates owns the restaurant and has personally sent you a note that says "Enjoy anything you like, on the house!" you're probably talking appetizers, several glasses of wine, any entree you want, dessert and an after-dinner drink. Or three.

It's a similar situation with Google Ad Grants. Let's take the very general issue of broad-match keywords. Earlier, we discussed how the use of broad-match keywords allows Google to be very liberal about when it chooses to show your ad. If you're bidding on the broad-match keyword of "running shoes," you might be inclined to think that your ad is going to show up only when people type "running shoes" into Google. But that's not the case.

Google may decide to also show your ad when people search for "running boards for a Chevy Silverado" (hey, they both have "running" in them, right?) or "tap dancing shoes" (hey, they both have "shoes" in there, right?). Because of this, broad-match keywords are known by all professional AdWords managers to be laden with pitfalls and waste.

But wait a second. Let's say that instead of a for-profit AdWords account, we're managing a Google Ad Grants account for a non-profit. And instead of trying NOT to spend a lot of money, we're actually given a pot of $329 each day that we MUST spend, or else it disappears.

Guess who has become our friend again all of a sudden? That's right: broad-match keywords.

In a perfect world, a nonprofit could use its Ad Grants account to bid only on the stronger, generally more fruitful exact match and phrase match keywords, and get tons of super-relevant traffic to its site. But honestly, that's unlikely to happen. Simply put, exact-match keywords command a higher cost per click and thus require a higher bid in order to trigger high-position ads on the search engine results pages (SERPs). And the $2 maximum bid constraint on Ad Grants accounts is rarely enough to get that done.

But our broad-match friends are great at spending money, and that's why broad-match keywords are a great idea for grants accounts. No, they aren't generally as relevant as the stronger match types, but when the stronger match types are prohibitively expensive, they're our next best option.

You might be inclined to ask why we'd want to employ the keywords that frequently attract those out-of-left-field, crazy, inappropriately matched search queries that I mentioned above. It's a good question, one that really gets at the heart of our philosophy about how the Google Ad Grants program should be viewed and used. That's a lovely segue into our next tip.

SPEND FIRST, STRIP LATER

Because the Ad Grant allocation is $329 per day and is use-it-or-lose it, we believe any traffic is better than no traffic, regardless of how irrelevant the search query may be. Let's begin with a purposely ludicrous example: A Google user searches for "winter coats under $29 made from purple unicorn hides." Now, let's say that for whatever reason, a broad-match keyword in your Google Ad Grants account triggers one of your nonprofit's ads to appear when this person is searching for his unicorn-skin coat. And that person, for a moment anyhow, is derailed from his equine outwear quest and decides to click on your ad to see what your nonprofit is all about.

Question 1: What's the likelihood that this seeker of unicorn coats is going to have a meaningful interest in your nonprofit? Well, we aren't sure about that, but judging by his search query, he's in the middle of researching a very, very specific product he wants to buy, and your nonprofit has nothing to do with that product. Why he clicked our ad is anyone's guess, but the safest bet is that this unicorn-coat buyer will not become a donor or a volunteer for you.

Question 2: Despite our pessimism about Unicorn Man, would we rather him visit our site, or would we rather have *no one* visit our site? I mean, Unicorn Man may turn out to have little value to us, but at least we exposed one more person to our site. Even if he's worthless to us, if it cost us just $1.50 of Google's $329 daily allotment of play money to bring him here, was it better that the money just stayed in our account all day and got flushed down the toilet by going unspent, never to be seen again?

Of course not. In a pinch, I'd rather spend my daily ad credit on probably irrelevant traffic than not spend it at all and leave it in Google's pocket. So our first order of business when we start managing an Ad Grants account is simple:

Let's spend this money.

Let's first get ourselves up to the point where we're hitting our $329 budget cap every single day; otherwise, we're wasting free money every day simply because we're not yet able to spend every dime of it on the "perfect customers": those 100% likely to donate money or time to our cause. Finding those people is hard and takes time; in the meantime, let's fling open the doors and invite the masses, washed and unwashed alike, into this party.

This is the "spend first" part of the equation. Above all things, let's spend the damn money already, because at midnight, it's gone and out of our lives forever, like Mary Swanson left Lloyd Christmas in "Dumb and Dumber" when she jumped on that plane to Aspen.

Once we're easily hitting our $329 per day worth of spending, it's time to switch gears. Now's the time to pull out the magnifying glass and look over the keywords that are bringing in our traffic and ask ourselves the following:

1. How much of our traffic is being generated by search queries that indicate a strong interest in what our nonprofit does? Obviously, this is what we want. Ideally, we want 100% of our traffic to fall squarely into this category. Let's say we run a nonprofit art museum in the city of Palookaville. Search queries like "art museums" or "Palookaville museums" are great queries. Those folks are who we're targeting. Good stuff.

2. By contrast, how much of our traffic looks like it originated with search queries indicating an interest in something altogether different from what we do? What about search queries like "The Art of Picking Up Women" or "Art Briles" (the Baylor University football coach who was fired due to a sexual assault scandal associated with his team)? Those are bad search queries – those queries absolutely are not made by Palookaville art lovers or potential museum visitors – so we don't want to waste our daily ad impressions on people searching for things like that. So we eliminate those queries via negative keywording in a process we call "stripping." We strip out the bad and leave the good.

3. After we've stripped out the bad queries, we've liberated some extra spending power from the account. The cost of clicks originating from irrelevant searches like "Art Briles" and "The Art of Picking Up Women" will no longer be

incurred, and that budget is now free to be used on the good queries you see in item A. Strip the bad and leave the good.

4. Lather, rinse, repeat. Checking your account for bad queries is a job that never truly ends. The universe of search queries employed by Google users exceeds anyone's imagination, and irrelevant ones will continue to seep into your account, sucking your spending power away from the good queries. Because of this, you should check your search queries weekly, at the very least. Scrub the bad and leave the good, and you'll be rewarded with a higher-performing, ever-more-relevant Ad Grants account.

USE KEYWORD TOOLS TO EXPAND YOUR ... LIKE ... KEYWORD MIND, MAN.

You've probably gotten the picture now that a big part of your success with Ad Grants is keywords, keywords, keywords. Go wide, right?

Well, it's hard to truly go wide without the help of some additional, external keyword tools. No one can sit down with pencil and paper and simply brainstorm hundreds of thousands of relevant search queries. Luckily, you don't have to. There are tools that will do it for you. Here are our favorites:

Ubersuggest.io

Ubersuggest.com was very popular for years, but then it died and disappeared (or at least stopped working). But it's been reborn as

Ubersuggest.io, and it works wonderfully. And not for nothing, it's free, and that's why it's at the top of our list.

To use Ubersuggest, you simply "seed" the tool with a basic search term to get it started – something very obviously related to your organization, so maybe "art museum" for our previous example – and it spits out the most popular Google searches containing those keywords. And with just a couple of clicks, you can select all the keywords you want to keep and download them onto your computer in an Excel file.

KeywordTool.io

This is also a great tool that works well and very similarly to Ubersuggest, although it's a distant second place for us because you only get a limited set of keywords and data unless you pay for the "Pro" version, which in our humble opinion is not worth its price tag of $88 a month. But one cool feature of KeywordTool.io is that you can query not only the most popular Google searches but the most popular searches on YouTube, Bing, Amazon and the iTunes App Store as well.

KeywordShitter.com

That's right, we said Keyword Shitter. We don't know who's behind Keyword Shitter and its primitive, toilet-themed web application, but we do know one thing: It works really, really well, and it's also free. Just plug your seed keywords into Keyword Shitter, click the "Shit Keywords!" button (I'm not joking), and Keyword Shitter will … well, excrete thousands of relevant keywords for you at light speed. If you just want to produce a giant list of keywords,

I'd recommend Keyword Shitter over Ubersuggest, even.

Found.co.uk Concatenation Tool

Found is a London-based search advertising agency we respect very much, and part of the reason we respect it so much is that it's built a fantastic and free keyword concatenation tool and made it available to the public. "Concatenation" for our purposes here means "putting together in every possible combination," and being able to do that for thousands of keywords in a fraction of a second is an incredible boon. Not only can you concatenate your keywords with this tool, you can also generate keywords across all of Google's match types in that same fraction of a second.

Let's put it this way: If we had to choose one of the four tools listed above to be stranded on a desert island with while trying to run StraightForward Interactive, it'd be the Found concatenation tool, without hesitation. You'll love it!

During keyword selection, think about user mindset and intent.

If you are like most AdWords newbies, the first set of keywords you generate will probably contain a lot of phrases that describe exactly what your nonprofit does. That seems like an OK place to start – indeed, every AdWords starter guide you ever come across will probably tell you to do so – but that's merely the beginning of your keyword generation process. To properly capture the attention of your target audience, you have to think about what they will be searching for when they're in need of services that you provide.

My favorite example to use is also our favorite type of non-profit to work for, and those are suicide-prevention organizations. They're our favorite because the work we do quite literally saves people's lives, and that's pretty rare in the dark, soulless pit of deception and half-truths known as the advertising industry.

It's our job to select keywords that people are searching for when they're considering taking their own lives. If we do our jobs well, our ads jump in front of that person at the most critical of moments, and if I can get them to click and then call a hotline, that's many times more rewarding than selling tickets to a fund-raiser concert or getting someone to pledge $100 for a fun run.

So let's take a look at a fictional organization that we'll call Suicide Hotline Inc. Bidding on words that generically describe precisely what it does, like "suicide prevention" or "suicide intervention services," is a good start, and it should definitely bid on those keywords. But it isn't going to reach a lot of people with those alone.

Why? Because that's what school administrators and teachers and volunteers and people like that search for when they're interested in learning about preventing suicide. It's not what people search for when they're actually suicidal and thinking about killing themselves at this very moment. They search for things like:

- painless ways to kill yourself
- how much benadryl do I have to take to die
- i don't want to live anymore

- where should i leave a suicide note
- where should i shoot myself to make sure i die
- i want to kill myself
- will i go to hell if i commit suicide

Those, and hundreds of thousands of similar searches. So that's what you need to be bidding on in order to effectively intervene with as many suicidal people as possible. In other words, you have to anticipate their mindset and intent. Put yourself in their shoes. What are the exact questions they'll be asking at the moment they need you the most?

Second example: If you're an adoption agency, don't just bid on "adoption services." Bid on "i'm pregnant what do i do," "abortion clinics near me," "unwanted pregnancy help" and the many thousands of iterations of those phrases. Frankly, we advise our adoption agency clients to bid on every pregnancy-related search they can generate, to get in front of as many pregnant women as possible.

In sum: Get in the mindset of the Google searcher who has the problem that your organization aims to help with, and anticipate the keywords they'll use to ask the oracle, Google, for solutions. Don't forget to use your keyword tools to help you!

Note: This is a good time to mention that our agency, StraightForward Interactive, provides Ad Grants management to suicide-prevention organizations free of charge. We mean no disrespect to the 99% of nonprofits out there that address other causes, but when our expertise can save lives, we want to do so, and we don't want any money for it. For more information, drop us a line at josh.barsch@gmail.com and stevelisaacs@gmail.com.

FREQUENTLY ASKED QUESTIONS

(Or, "Everything You Wanted to Know About Google Ad Grants but Were
Too Much of a Trembling Wallflower to Ask")

Over the years, we've been asked lots of questions about Google
Ad Grants by nonprofit leaders. Most of those questions are the
same dozen or so, asked over and over again, so that tells us an
FAQ section is in order.

**What happens when you've spent $329 in a day? Do you have
to turn your ads off?**

No. Once your spending for a given day hits the max of $329,
your ads will be automatically be shut off by Google and will no
longer run for the remainder of that day. They'll resume running
again at midnight (or, if you're using a custom ad schedule, at the
regularly scheduled time the following day).

What happens if we go over the $329 daily limit in a day?

That's very unlikely, other than by a dollar or two, which is fine.
Back in the old days of the program, it was theoretically possible
for you to rack up spending far beyond the $329 per day (and

thus place yourself at risk of being kicked out of the program). This is no longer the case; now, your ads will automatically stop running when the account hits a total of $329 in spending. Every once in a great, great while – I'd say once a year, maximum – we see a glitch in the AdWords system that allows an extra $50 to $100 in daily spend to slip through in a single day. But that's extremely rare, and we've never seen any consequences from that. Our best guess is that it's Google's own glitch, it gets fixed, and the company takes responsibility for that.

How many different things can you promote with your Ad Grants account at one time?

There's no limit to how many pages of your website that you can promote with your Ad Grants account. You can promote one thing or 100 things; it's entirely up to you.

What happens if I apply for Google for Nonprofits and I'm denied? Can I reapply?

Yes, you can, but your chances are slim. Approval for the Google for Nonprofits programs is generally automatic and nearly instantaneous; if you've been rejected, that means Google has found some indication that your entire organization is ineligible for its suite of nonprofit benefits. But if, for example, you mistyped your tax ID number in your initial application, you should definitely reapply; in that case, Google was using bad information in its approval process, and the correct information should yield better results. But if Google has decreed that you're an ineligible organization the first time around, reapplying is unlikely to change that.

How often do I have to make changes to my account in order to keep the Grant?

Once every 90 days, minimum. If you're self-managing and you don't know really know much about AdWords, just log in and change a handful of your $2.00 bids to $1.99. That'll keep you out of trouble.

Some of my keywords have statuses of "Below First Page Minimum Bid" or "Low Search Volume." What should I do?

There's not much you can do to change either of these things, so the best course of action is to do nothing. "Low Search Volume" is simply Google telling you that very few people search for this particular phrase, and until more people start doing so, it's not going to display your ads when people do. You are completely powerless to change this, so don't worry about it.

"Below First Page Minimum Bid" means just that: Your $2 bid isn't high enough to get you on the first page of search results. You can't change that either, because you're not allowed to increase your bids above $2, so don't worry about it. However, a silver lining there: A lot of times, that's simply false. We have keywords in many of our accounts that, despite carrying "Below First Page" status, get hundreds of impressions daily. So, don't lose any sleep over it.

My organization had a Google Ad Grant in the past, but we can't access it. What now?

This situation is unfortunately common, and often – not always, but often – there's no happy ending. That's due to one clause that's been in the Ad Grants agreement since the program's inception: the "no set-it-and-forget-it" rule. As you read earlier, Google's rule for the Ad Grants program is that you must actively manage your account, and its yardstick of active management is that at least one change to the account must be made every 90 days.

In our experience, when a nonprofit comes to us and indicates that it once had a Google Ad Grants account but now has no access, can't find it, etc., it's usually a situation in which far more than 90 days have passed since anyone in the organization has touched it. It's far more common to hear something like this: "I know we had a Grants account a few years ago, but it was Tim the IT guy who set it up, and he hasn't worked here for 18 months!"

So that usually means that it's been a hell of a lot longer than 90 days since anyone's made a change to the account and that you've probably been kicked out of the program for violating this rule. And once you've been kicked out of the program, it's nearly impossible to get back in. My agency has worked with hundreds of nonprofits over the years, and there's been exactly one time when we were able to get an expelled nonprofit back into the program. And honestly, this was due to a perfect storm of factors, good luck being chief among them: Our long history with Google, a very friendly Google rep who happened to like us a great deal, a somewhat high-profile nonprofit client and a very, very good "sob story" from an extremely personable and convincing Mr. Steve Isaacs. Without any one of those things, I don't think we could've retrieved that one, either.

However: If this is the situation you're in, it's not 100% hopeless. The saving grace of many nonprofits in similar straits is the fact that, as I've mentioned before in this book, the Google Ad Grants team is lightly staffed, and its program rules are not always strictly enforced. And sometimes, when they are enforced, they're very slowly enforced. For example, the 90-day account change rule is not automatic/algorithmic (at least not yet) – that is to say, there seems to be no script or automated process Google uses to immediately shut off inactive accounts on Day 91 of inactivity. We know this because we've taken over accounts with six months, nine months and, on rare occasions, even a year of inactivity, and they've still been live and spending money. This means that somewhere behind the scenes at Google, it takes a conscious decision from a sentient human being to strike the death blow and expel a nonprofit from the program due to inactivity.

In sum: Just because you're certain that 90 days have passed without active management doesn't mean your account is dead and banned. You want to get access to it as soon as you can so that you can make quick changes and reset your 90-day clock as soon as humanly possible – before Google realizes that its alarm clock to ban your account has been buzzing for months!

Finding an old Ad Grants account is easier said than done, and doing so is an inexact science. Here's the process we find works best.

1. First, ask around the office. Every Ad Grant is associated with someone's email address, and that someone is usually

the person who set up the Ad Grant in the first place.

2. If that person is now gone from the organization but you can still contact him/her, do so. Ask what email they used to set up the grant and whether they still have access to it. If they do, they can log into the account and grant administrative privileges to a current employee of your organization.

3. If that person can't be found – or even identified – check through the old email in the inboxes of your organization's "generic" email addresses – I'm talking about email addresses like info@, contact@, things like that. If these inboxes are searchable, search for "AdWords," which will appear in any communication you have from Google about your Ad Grants account.

4. If all of this fails, call 866-2-GOOGLE and cross your fingers that you get a helpful rep. Tell them that you have a Google Ad Grants account, that your organization has lost track of its whereabouts and that you really need to access it so that you don't lose your grant. Your mileage may vary, but it's worth a last-gasp effort.

Can religious organizations get a Google Ad Grant?

Yes! As long as you're a 501(c)(3) and meet all other Ad Grant requirements, religious organizations are eligible. If you're headquartered outside the US and hold valid charity status in your country of origin (Google has guidelines for each country on what holding "valid charity status" entails), you're eligible. However, one additional thing is worth mentioning here: Any organization that discriminates in its hiring/employment practices based on sexual orientation or gender identity is not eligible for a Google

Ad Grant. Even if your nonprofit has religious reasons for doing so, and even if doing so is entirely legal in your area, you're not eligible for a Google Ad Grant if your hiring practices restrict employment based on these factors.

Even churches?

Yes, even churches. If your church is registered as a 501(c)(3) or holds valid charity status outside the US and meets all the other program guidelines, your church will be eligible. See the above question about religious organizations.

Do I need to capitalize proper nouns in my keyword lists?

No. Keywords are not case-sensitive, so "Georgia" and "georgia" are duplicates, as far as Google is concerned.

Should I ever set my bids lower than $2?

Great question! Usually, you'll want to leave them at $2, because, all else being equal, higher bids equal higher ad positions, and higher ad positions equal more clicks. But what if you're one of those lucky nonprofits whose keywords generate millions of queries daily and attract so many clicks that their $329 allotment is fully spent before noon? In that case, we drop our clients' bids, and sometimes quite steeply. But why?

Well, we've got $329 per day to spend. And let's say our $2 bids are generating clicks that cost us, on average, $1.50 each (that's not unusual; only very rarely will your clicks actually cost you the full $2 apiece, even if you're bidding $2). OK, $329 a day gets us about 220 clicks at $1.50 a pop. Not bad. But if search volume is heavy and we're spending up our allotment early in the day, we should ask ourselves: What if we dropped our bids to, say, $1 per click instead of $2? Yes, our ads will probably drop in position, and our clickthrough rates will fall. That's the downside. But what if our bid reduction also drops our average cost per click down to, let's say, 75 cents? Wouldn't we then get 440 clicks to our website each day for the same $329 we were spending to get 220 clicks before?

Absolutely, and in cases like that, it's a very savvy move to drop your bids. Please note, though: This works only when the flood of traffic – and by that I mean, the number of people out there searching for your keywords – is so heavy that even a steep drop in your ad position won't stop hundreds of people from clicking on your ads every day. This strategy can certainly be taken too far. Let's say you decided to drop your bids from $2.00 per click all the way to 10 cents per click, in the hopes that you can generate $329 worth of 10-cent clicks every day, allowing you to squeeze 3,290 new visitors into your site each day with the Ad Grant.

Not gonna happen, my friend. A 10-cent bid will yield ad position so dismally low that your ads won't even appear until the second or third page of search results – pages we know most folks never even see. You'll end up with zilch: no ad impressions, no clicks and no visitors.

But if you're in this situation – heavy traffic on your keywords, heavy clicks on your ads and no problem whatsoever hitting your daily max spend – feel free to experiment with your bids. For example, drop everything to $1.50 and see what happens the next couple days. If the strategy works and more and more clicks roll in, lower 'em again, maybe to $1. Lather, rinse, repeat. You'll eventually find Google's version of what economists call "pricing equilibrium": that point where your bid price roughly matches the maximum number of folks you can get clicking up $329 worth of your budget each day.

What happens if I apply for a Google Ad Grant and I'm denied? Can I reapply?

Yes, you can. If you have been accepted into the Google for Non-profits program – the umbrella program under which Ad Grants is one of several offerings – a rejection for Ad Grants isn't too big of a deal. It probably means you've simply made a mistake in setting up your AdWords account. The most common ways to mess this up are:

1. You checked the box that said "include Search Partners" in one of your ad campaigns. (You're not allowed to use Search Partners with an Ad Grants account.)
2. You chose a Bid Strategy other than "Manual CPC" in one of your ad campaigns. (Of the many bid strategies available to AdWords advertisers, only Manual CPC can be used with Ad Grants accounts.)
3. You checked the "Enhanced CPC" button when you set up one of your ad campaigns (you're not allowed to use Enhanced CPC with Google Ad Grants.)
4. You didn't include at least one ad and one keyword in your first ad group.

If you've been rejected, go back and check these items. Chances are, you've just made an oversight and botched one of these things. Fix it, then follow the instructions in your rejection email for how to resubmit (a couple of clicks is all it takes).

We are a nonprofit, but we're a 501(c)(6), not a 501(c)(3). Can we get a Google Ad Grant?

No. 501(c)(6) organizations – the IRS "business league" classification of nonprofit organizations that includes chambers of commerce, real estate boards, etc. – are not eligible for Google Ad Grants. Only 501(c)(3) organizations are eligible.

We're a nonprofit, but we're not based in the United States. Are we eligible for an Ad Grant?

Possibly. As of this writing, the Google Ad Grants program is available for nonprofits registered in the following countries: Argentina, Australia, Austria, Belgium, Botswana, Brazil, Bulgaria, Canada, Chile, Colombia, Croatia, Czech Republic, Denmark, Egypt, Finland, France, Germany, Hong Kong, Hungary, India, Indonesia, Ireland, Israel, Italy, Japan, Kenya, Korea, Luxembourg, Macau, Malaysia, Mexico, Netherlands, New Zealand, Norway, Philippines, Poland, Romania, Russia, Serbia, Singapore, Slovakia, Slovenia, South Africa, Spain, Sweden, Switzerland, Taiwan, Thailand, Turkey, United Kingdom, United States and Vietnam.

We're a nonprofit with separate chapters in foreign countries. Can each of our entities get a Google Ad Grant?

Yes, you can. Let's say Acme Dog Rescue is headquartered in France and has created nonprofits called Acme USA, Acme

Australia and Acme Mexico, each a separate organization registered in its respective country. All three of these organizations are eligible for their own Google Ad Grant. For this reason, if your mission is international and you have boots on the ground in multiple countries, you should definitely weigh the costs and benefits of setting up separate organizations in each country. $10,000 per month in free advertising for each organization can go a long way toward explosive growth!

We've filed our nonprofit paperwork with the IRS, but it hasn't been processed. Can we apply for an Ad Grant?

No, you must wait until the IRS has processed your paperwork and officially granted nonprofit status upon you before applying for an Ad Grant. (The application process automatically queries your IRS NTEE code, and if your paperwork isn't processed, you won't have a code, so you'll be rejected.)

We're a local chapter of a larger regional (or national, or international) nonprofit, with whom we share the same tax ID number. Are we eligible for our own Google Ad Grant here at our local office?

Yes! Although Google for Nonprofits allows only one membership per organization, branches of "umbrella organizations" that have the same EIN as their parent organizations are eligible for individual Ad Grants. In your application, you must indicate that you're applying as a "related organization" underneath your parent organization (you can do this in a free-form comment box inside the application). Google will do a little sniffing out of whether you truly are a part of your mothership organization, and once it's done that, you should receive your Ad Grant.

For large organizations, this is an incredibly beneficial feature of the program. Take the American Diabetes Association. It's a large national organization, but it also has local "suborganizations" based on geography, such as the ADA of Colorado, the ADA of Minnesota, etc. There are more than 50 of these local affiliates, and each one is eligible for its own $10,000 a month Ad Grant. If each affiliate uses its Ad Grant, that's over $500,000 in free advertising for the ADA each month. Incredible!

MARCHING ORDERS

(Or, "What to Do Next")

Well, here we are, nearing the end of the book. If you read everything up to this point, we congratulate you: There's a lot of information packed into these pages, enough to make your head spin. But we hope you've come away with a lot of new ideas about how Google Ad Grants can help you grow.

The case we've tried to make in this book is that Ad Grants is definitely worth doing. But to reap the benefits, you've got to do it well, and if the previous pages have shown you anything, it's that doing it well takes a great deal of time and effort.

Below, we'll explore your two options for building your Ad Grants account into a well-oiled growth machine: doing it yourself or hiring an agency. But first things first: If your organization isn't enrolled in Google for Nonprofits, sign up right away at www.google.com/nonprofits. Even with Google's irksome requirement that all nonprofits be validated via the TechSoup organization, it should take you 15 minutes, max.

Once that's done, you've got a decision to make about how to move forward with your Ad Grants account.

1. **Do it yourself.** You know what's coming after the do-it-yourself choice, and that's the hiring-an-agency choice, and you know that your trusty authors here run just such an agency and that we'd love to have more business. But now that we've addressed that big fat elephant in the room, make no mistake: You absolutely can do it yourself. We know that for sure. This book is a blueprint for running a successful, maxed-out Ad Grants account, and if you follow the teachings here, you can do it.

   What we don't know is whether you have the time. Anyone can follow the individual steps in our guidebook, but not everyone can put aside the hours every week required to do so – and that doesn't include the hours it takes to familiarize yourself with the inner workings of Google AdWords that you really need to know if you truly want to maximize your grant.

   If you or someone on your staff is somewhat familiar with the tools required to build a successful Google AdWords account, you might be able to go it alone here. Or, if you're one of those lucky souls who really does have plenty of time left over each week to devote hours to learning a new trade, it might work for you, too.

   If you choose this route, DON'T FORGET: Once your

Ad Grant is live, you are on Google's "active-management" clock and must make changes to your account on a regular basis. If you aren't certain that you have the in-house resources to handle doing optimizations at least once every 90 days, don't apply. Wait until you do. It's better to wait than to jump in whole-hog, get your grant and then lose it forever because you didn't have the human resources available to meet the active-management requirement.

But if you're a completely newbie to Google AdWords and you're already pressed for time in your week, you should give some consideration to hiring out.

2. **Hire an agency.** The greatest aspect of a Google Ad Grant is, of course, its cost. It's free! And nothing beats free, right?

Maybe so, but remember our analogy of the Cadillac with no engine. Google will give you $10,000 worth of free advertising, but unless you know how to actually spend the $10,000, it won't get spent, and your organization can't benefit. It's a Cadillac with no engine.

That's not just a sales pitch from a guy who, admittedly, has a vested interest in selling his agency's Ad Grants management services. Remember our earlier stat: The average self-managed Ad Grants account actually ends up spending a measly $300 to $500 per month in advertising credit out of the $10,000 it's given. Ouch!

So unless you're fortunate enough to have a Google AdWords wizard in-house, there's a strong case to be made for having professionals manage your account. An agency specializing in Google Ad Grants management is familiar with how to navigate all the difficulties and pitfalls of a Grants account and can help you maximize your grant usage every month.

The next question, of course, is cost. If you're paying an agency to manage your Ad Grants account, you're paying them with cash money, not Google advertising credit. Naturally, you'll have to decide how much actual money from your marketing budget it's worth to get that $10,000 per month in advertising credit used to best effect. And obviously, the less you pay for that expertise, the more palatable a financial decision it becomes to hire the experts.

At StraightForward, we charge $400 per month. That's the lowest price I've ever seen charged by an agency that's truly a specialist with deep experience with Google Ad Grants. And frankly, that's why we set our prices so low in the first place: to make our offering the best one on the market for Ad Grants management. I've seen agencies that charge $500, $700, $1,500 and just about everything in between. I've also seen some very small players – overseas contractors, one-person home-based start-ups, etc. – charge as little as $200, but it's been my experience that these outfits have little to no experience with the unique complexities and demands of an Ad Grants account.

If you're interested in having our team at StraightForward Interactive handle your Ad Grants management, we'd love to have you. Drop us a note at josh.barsch@gmail.com and stevelisaacs@gmail.com. Those are our real, personal email addresses. Ask anything you like. We're here to help.

EPILOGUE

(Or, "You Can Close the Book Now. It's Over.")

We aren't ones to overstay our welcome, so we'll be going now.

We hope you enjoyed the book and it gets you excited about the possibilities that a well-managed Google Ad Grant can bring to your nonprofit.

You've got the tools and the playbook. Good luck, and thanks for buying our book!

All the best,
Josh & Steve

71193743R00088

31192021264260

Made in the USA
Columbia, SC
Iay 2017